The Psychology of the Esoteric

the text of this book is printed on 100% recycled paper

Other books by Bhagwan Shree Rajneesh available from Harper & Row*:

I Am the Gate: Initiation and Discipleship
Meditation: The Art of Ecstasy
The Book of the Secrets
The Mustard Seed

* A complete list of his books in English is available through Rajneesh Foundation, 17 Koregaon Park, Poona, India.

Bhagwan Shree Rajneesh

The Psychology of the Esoteric

Edited by Ma Satya Bharti

HARPER COLOPHON BOOKS
Harper & Row, Publishers
New York, Hagerstown, San Francisco, London

This work was first published in the English language in India under the title *The Inward Revolution*.

FIRST U.S. EDITION: Harper Colophon Books, 1978

ISBN: 0-06-090616-2

Designed by Stephanie Krasnow

79 80 81 82 10 9 8 7 6 5 4 3 2

Contents

Introduction

The evolutionary process is a process in the development of consciousness. Trees are more conscious than rocks; animals are more conscious than trees; man is more conscious than animals; Buddhas are more conscious than man. Buddhahood, Christ-consciousness, enlightenment, all mean the same thing: the flowering of total consciousness. Matter is totally unconscious; a Buddha is totally conscious. Man is somewhere in between: neither this nor that. He lives in a state of limbo. No longer an animal and not yet a god. No longer what he was and not yet that which he can become.

"Unconscious evolution ends with man," Bhagwan tells us, "and conscious evolution begins. But conscious evolution doesn't necessarily begin in any particular man. It begins only if you choose it to begin."

Life means movement. It's impossible to remain where we are. Either we evolve to a higher level of consciousness or we regress. The choice is ours. We can't not-choose. Even not choosing is a subtle choice. Most people seek oblivion: a return to unconsciousness. They seek it through alcohol and drugs, through work, through sex, through sensory stimulation. Only a few choose to begin the journey toward higher consciousness. It's to these few that Bhagwan addresses the discourses contained in *The Psychology of the Esoteric.*

Bhagwan begins from the point where Western psychology leaves off. He goes beyond Freud, beyond Jung, beyond the new understandings of the human potential movement. If Freud's psychology is a psychology of pathology and Maslow's psychology is a psychology of the healthy man, Bhagwan's psychology is a psychology of enlightenment, of Buddhahood. Bhagwan is not only an enlightened Master; he is also a master psychologist. He unpeels the layers of our being, revealing the inner depths that lay hidden within us. He starts from the physical and moves step by step to the transcendental. He starts from the known and moves to the unknowable. He starts from where we are to take us to where we can be. "In the East," he says, "it's not a question of psychology; it's a question of being. It's not a question of mental health. Rather, it's a question of spiritual growth. The question is not what you do; the question is what you are."

What Bhagwan is talking about in these discourses is nothing less than the creation of a new man. His whole effort is to create a climate in which Buddhahood can begin to flower. For that to happen, he says, we must accept man in his totality. Neither the rational must be denied nor the irrational; neither the intellect nor the emotions; neither the scientific nor the religious. Man must remain flowing, fluid, capable of moving from one pole to the other. "The mind must be trained in a logical, rational way," he says, "but it must simultaneously be trained in irrational (non-rational) meditation. The reason must be trained and at the same time the emotions. Doubt must be there, but faith also. . . . Neither one who has denied the irrational nor one who has denied the rational is growing. You can't grow unless you grow totally."

Bhagwan is not a philosopher. His words aren't an attempt to fill our minds with more knowledge. They're an attempt to push us toward a direct experience of that-which-is-beyond-words. They're an attempt to push us toward our own inner evolution. The ultimate realization of our potential. The potentiality of our seed.

ma satya bharti

1

Inward Revolution

On man's path of evolution is it possible that at some time in the future humanity as a whole can attain enlightenment? At what point of evolution is man today?

With man, the natural, automatic process of evolution ends. Man is the last product of unconscious evolution. With man, conscious evolution begins.

Many things are to be taken into account. First, unconscious evolution is mechanical and natural. It happens by itself. Through this type of evolution, consciousness evolves. But the moment consciousness comes into being, unconscious evolution stops because its purpose has been fulfilled. Unconscious evolution is needed only up to the point where the conscious comes into being.

Man has become conscious. In a way, he has transcended nature. Now nature cannot do anything; the last product that was possible through natural evolution has come into being. Now man becomes free to decide whether to evolve or not to evolve.

Secondly, unconscious evolution is collective, but the moment evolution becomes conscious it becomes individual. No collective, automatic evolution proceeds further than mankind. From now on, evolution becomes an individual process. Consciousness creates individuality. Before consciousness evolves, there is no individuality. Only species exist, not individuality.

When evolution is still unconscious, it is an automatic process; there is no uncertainty about it. Things happen through the law of cause and effect. Existence is mechanical and certain. But with man, with consciousness, uncertainty comes into existence. Now, nothing is certain. Evolution may take place or it may not. The potential is there, but the choice will rest entirely with each individual.

That is why anxiety is a human phenomenon. Below man there is no anxiety because there is no choice. Everything happens as it must. There is no choice so there is no chooser, and in the absence of the chooser, anxiety is impossible. Who is to be anxious? Who is to be tense?

With the possibility of choice, anxiety follows like a shadow. Everything has to be chosen now; everything is a conscious effort. You alone are responsible. If you fail, you fail. It is your responsibility. If you succeed, you succeed. It is again your responsibility.

And every choice is ultimate in a sense. You cannot undo it, you cannot forget it, you cannot go back on it. Your choice becomes your destiny. It will remain with you and be a part of you; you cannot deny it. But your choice is always a gamble. Every choice is made in darkness because nothing is certain. That is why man suffers from anxiety. He is anxious to his very roots. What torments him, to begin with, is: to be or not to be? to do or not to do? to do this or to do that?

"No choice" is not possible. If you do not choose, then you are choosing not to choose; it is a choice. So you are forced to choose; you are not free not to choose. Not choosing will have as much effect as any other choice.

Thc dignity, the beauty and the glory of man is this consciousness. But it is a burden also. The glory and the burden come simultaneously the minute you become conscious. Every step is a movement between the two. With man, choice and conscious individuality come into existence. You can evolve, but your evolution will be an individual endeavor. You may evolve to become a Buddha or you may not. The choice is yours.

So there are two types of evolution: collective evolution and individual, conscious evolution. "Evolution" implies unconscious, collective progress, so it would be better to use the word "revolution" in talking about man. With man, revolution becomes possible. Revolution, as I am using the word here, means a conscious, individual effort toward evolution. It is bringing individual responsibility to a peak. Only you are responsible for your own evolution.

Ordinarily, man tries to escape from his responsibility for his own evolution, from the responsibility of freedom of choice. There is a great fear of freedom. When you are a slave the responsibility for your life is never yours; someone else is responsible. So in a way, slavery is a very comfortable thing. There is no burden. In this respect, slavery is a freedom: freedom from conscious choice.

The moment you become completely free, you have to make your own choices. No one forces you to do anything; all alternatives are open to you. Then the struggle with the mind begins. So one becomes afraid of freedom.

Part of the appeal of ideologies such as communism and fascism is that they provide an escape from individual freedom and a shirking of individual responsibility. The burden of responsibility is taken away from the individual; the society becomes responsible. When something goes wrong, you can always point to the state, the organization. Man becomes just a part of the collective structure. But in denying individual freedom, fascism and communism also deny the possibility of human evolution. It is a falling back from the great possibility that revolution offers: the total transformation of human beings. When this happens, you destroy the possibility of achieving the ultimate. You fall back; you again become like animals.

To me, further evolution is possible only with individual responsibility. You alone are responsible! This responsibility is a great blessing in disguise. With this individual responsibility comes the struggle that ultimately leads to choiceless awareness.

The old pattern of unconscious evolution has ended for us. You can fall back into it, but you cannot remain in it. Your being will revolt. Man has become conscious; he has to remain conscious. There is no other way.

Philosophers like Aurobindo have great appeal for escapists. They say that collective evolution is possible. The divine will descend and everyone will become enlightened. But to me that is not possible. And even if it appears possible, it is not worthwhile. If you become enlightened without your own individual effort, then that enlightenment is not worth having. It will not give you the ecstasy that crowns the effort. It will just be taken for granted—like your eyes, your hands, your breathing system. These are great blessings, but no one really values them, cherishes them.

One day you can also be born with enlightenment, just as Aurobindo promises. It will be valueless. You will have much, but because it has come to you without effort, without toil, it will mean nothing to you; its significance will be lost. Conscious effort is necessary. The achievement is not as significant as the effort itself. Effort gives it its meaning, struggle gives it its significance.

As I see it, enlightenment that comes collectively, unconsciously, as a gift from the divine, is not only impossible but also meaningless. You must struggle for enlightenment. Through struggle, you create the capacity to see and feel and hold on to the bliss that comes.

Unconscious evolution ends with man and conscious evolution (revolution) begins. But conscious evolution does not necessarily begin in any particular man. It begins only if you choose it to begin. But if you do not choose it—as most people do not—you will be in a very tense condition. And present-day humanity is like this: nowhere to go, nothing to be achieved. Nothing can be achieved now without conscious effort. You cannot go back to a state of unconsciousness. The door has closed; the bridge has been broken.

The conscious choice to evolve is a great adventure, the only adventure there is for a human being. The path is arduous; it is bound to be so. Errors are bound to be there, failures, because nothing is certain. This situation creates tension in the mind. You do not know where you are, you do not know where you are going. Your identity is lost.

The situation may even reach such a point that you become suicidal. Suicide is a human phenomenon; it comes with human choice. Animals cannot commit suicide, because to choose death consciously is impossible for them. Birth is unconscious, death is unconscious. But with man—ignorant man, unevolved man—one thing becomes possible: the ability to choose death.

Your birth is not your choice. As far as your birth is concerned, you are in the hands of unconscious evolution. In fact, your birth is not a human happening at all. It is animal in nature, because it is not your choice. Only with choice does humanity begin. But you can choose your death—a decisive act. So suicide becomes a definite human act.

And if you do not choose conscious evolution, there is every possibility that you may choose to commit suicide. You may not have the courage actively to commit suicide but you will go through a slow, prolonged process of suicide—lingering, waiting to die.

You cannot make anyone else responsible for your evolution. To accept this situation gives you strength. You are on your way to growing, to evolving.

We create gods, or we take refuge in gurus, so that we will not have to be responsible for our own lives, for our own evolution. We try to place the responsibility somewhere else, away from us. If we are not able to accept some god or some guru, then we try to escape from responsibility through intoxicants or drugs, through anything that will make us unconscious. But these efforts to deny responsibility are absurd, juvenile, childish. They only postpone the problem; they are not solutions. You can postpone until death, but the problem still remains, and your new birth will continue in the same way.

Once you become aware that you alone are responsible, there is no escape through any type of unconsciousness. And you are foolish if you try to escape, because responsibility is a great opportunity for evolution. Out of the struggle that is created, something new may evolve.

To become aware means to know that everything depends on you. Even your god depends on you, because he is created by your imagination. Everything is ultimately a part of you, and you are responsible for it. There is no one to listen to your excuses; there are no courts of appeal. The whole responsibility is yours.

And you are alone, absolutely alone. This has to be understood very clearly. The moment a person becomes conscious, he becomes alone. The greater the consciousness, the greater the awareness that you are alone. So, do not escape from this fact through society, friends, associations, crowds. Do not escape from it! It is a great phenomenon; the whole process of evolution has been working toward this. Consciousness has come to the point now where you know that you are alone. And only in aloneness can you attain enlightenment.

I am not saying *loneliness*. The feeling of loneliness is the feeling that comes when one is escaping from aloneness, when one is not ready to accept it. If you do not accept the fact of aloneness, then you will feel lonely. Then you will find some crowd or some means of intoxication in which to forget yourself. Loneliness will create its own magic of forgetfulness.

If you can be *alone* even for a single moment, *totally alone*, the ego will die; the "I" will die. You will explode; you will be no more. The ego cannot remain alone. It can exist only in relation to others. Whenever you are alone, a miracle happens. The ego becomes weak. Now it cannot continue to exist for long. So if you can be courageous enough to be alone, you will gradually become egoless.

To be alone is a very conscious and deliberate act, more deliberate than suicide, because the ego cannot exist alone; but it can exist in suicide. Egoistic people are more prone to suicide. Suicide is always in relation to someone else; it is never an act of aloneness. In suicide, the ego will not suffer. Rather, it will become more expressive. It will enter into a new birth with greater force.

Through aloneness, the ego is shattered. It has nothing to relate to, so it cannot exist. So if you are ready to be alone, unwaveringly alone—neither escaping nor falling back, just accepting the fact of aloneness as it is—it becomes a great opportunity. Then you are just like a seed that has much potential in it. But remember, the seed must destroy itself for the plant to grow. Ego is a seed, a potentiality. If it is shattered, the divine is born. The divine is neither "I" nor "thou," it is *one*. Through aloneness, you come to this oneness.

You can create false substitutes for this oneness. Hindus become one, Christians become one, Mohammedans become one; India is one, China is one. These are just substitutes for oneness. Oneness comes only through total aloneness.

A crowd can call itself one, but the oneness is always in opposition to something else. Since the crowd is with you, you are at ease. Now you are not responsible any more. You would not burn a mosque alone, you would not destroy a temple alone, but as part of a crowd you can do it, because now you are not individually responsible. Everyone is responsible, so no one in particular is responsible. There is no individual consciousness, only a group consciousness. You regress in a crowd and become like an animal.

The crowd is a false substitute for the feeling of oneness. One who is aware of the situation, aware of his responsibility as a human being, aware of the difficult, arduous task that comes with being human, does not choose any false substitutes. He lives with the facts as they are; he does not create any fictions. Your religions and your political ideologies are just fictions, creating an illusory feeling of oneness.

Oneness comes only when you become egoless, and the ego can die only when you are totally alone. When you are completely alone, you are not. That very moment is the moment of explosion. You explode into the infinite. This, and only this, is evolution. I call it revolution because it is not unconscious. You may become egoless or you may not. It is up to you.

To be alone is the only real revolution. Much courage is needed. Only a Buddha is alone, only a Jesus or a Mahavir is alone. It is not that they left their families, left the world. It looks that way but it is not. They were not negatively leaving somehing. The act was positive; it was a movement toward aloneness. They were not leaving. They were in search of being totally alone.

The whole search is for that moment of explosion when one is alone. In aloneness there is bliss. And only then is enlightenment achieved.

We cannot be alone, others also cannot be alone, so we create groups, families, societies, nations. All nations, all families, all groups are made up of cowards, of those who are not courageous enough to be alone.

Real courage is the courage to be alone. It means a conscious realization of the fact that you *are* alone and you cannot be otherwise. You can either deceive yourself or you can live with this fact. You can continue deceiving yourself for lives and lives, but you will just go on in a vicious circle. Only if you can live with this fact of aloneness is the circle broken and you come to the center. That center is the center of divineness, of the whole, the holy.

I cannot conceive of a time when every human being will be able to achieve this as a birthright. It is impossible. Consciousness is individual. Only unconsciousness is collective. Human beings have come to the point of consciousness where they have become individuals. There is no humanity as such; there are only individual human beings. Each human being must realize his own individuality and the responsibility for it.

The first thing we must do is to accept aloneness as a basic fact and learn to live with it. We must not create any fictions. If you create fictions you will never be able to know the truth. Fictions are projected, created, cultivated truths that prevent you from knowing what is. Live with the fact of your aloneness. If you can live with this fact, if there is no fiction between you and this fact, then the truth will be revealed to you. Every fact, if looked into deeply, reveals the truth.

So live with the fact of responsibility, with the fact that you are alone. If you can live with this fact, the explosion will happen. It is arduous, but it is the only way. Through difficulty, through accepting this truth, you reach the point of explosion. Only then is there bliss. If it is given to you ready-made, it loses its worth because you have not earned it. You do not have the capacity to feel the bliss. This capacity comes only from discipline.

If you can live with the fact of your responsibility for yourself, a discipline will automatically come to you. By being totally responsible for yourself, you cannot help but become disciplined. But this discipline is not something forced upon you from the outside. It comes from within. Because of the total responsibility you carry for yourself, each step you take is disciplined. You cannot utter even one word irresponsibly.

If you are aware of your own aloneness, you will be aware of the anguish of others also. Then you will not be able to commit a single irresponsible act, because you will feel responsible not only for yourself but for others also. If you can live with the fact of your aloneness, you know that everyone is lonely. Then the son knows that the father is lonely; the wife knows that the husband is lonely; the husband knows that the wife is lonely. Once you know this, it is impossible not to be compassionate.

Living with facts is the only yoga, the only discipline. Once you are totally aware of the human situation, you become religious. You become a master of yourself. But the austerity that comes is not the austerity of an ascetic. It is not forced; it is not ugly. The austerity is aesthetic. You feel that it is the only thing possible, that you cannot do otherwise. Then you renounce things; you become nonpossessive.

The urge to possess is the urge not to be alone. One cannot be alone, so he seeks company. But the company of other people is not reliable, so he seeks, instead, the company of things. To live with a wife is difficult; to live with a car is not so difficult. So ultimately, possessiveness turns toward things.

You may even try to change persons into things. You try to mold them in such a way that they lose their personalities, their individuality. A wife is a thing, not a person; a husband is a thing, not a person.

If you become aware of your aloneness, then you become aware of the aloneness of others also. Then you know that to try to possess another is trespassing. You never positively renounce. Renunciation becomes the negative shadow of your aloneness. You become nonpossessive. Then you can be a lover, but not a husband, not a wife.

With this nonpossessiveness comes compassion and austerity. Innocence comes to you. When you deny the facts of life, you cannot be innocent; you become cunning. You deceive yourself and others. But if you are courageous enough to live with the facts as they are, you become innocent. This innocence is not cultivated. You are it: innocent.

To me, to be innocent is all that is to be achieved. Be innocent, and the divine is always blissfully flowing toward you. Innocence is the capacity to receive, to be part of the divine. Be innocent, and the guest is there. Become the host.

This innocence cannot be cultivated because cultivation is always a contrivance. It is calculated. But innocence can never be calculated; it is impossible.

Innocence is religiousness. To be innocent is the peak of true realization. But true innocence comes only through a conscious revolution; it is not possible through any collective, unconscious evolution. Man is alone. He is free to choose heaven or hell, life or death, the ecstasy of realization or the misery of our so-called life.

Sartre said somewhere: "Man is condemned to be free." You may choose either heaven or hell. Freedom means the freedom to choose either. If you can choose only heaven, then it is not a choice; it is not freedom. Heaven without the choice of hell will be hell itself. Choice always means either/or. It does not mean you are free to choose good only. Then there would be no freedom.

If you choose wrongly, freedom becomes a condemnation; but if you choose rightly, it becomes bliss. It depends on you whether your choice turns your freedom into condemnation or into bliss. The choice is totally your responsibility.

If you are ready, then from within your depths a new dimension can begin: the dimension of revolution. Evolution has ended. Now a revolution is needed to open you up to what is beyond. It is an individual revolution. An inward revolution.

2

Entering the Gap: The Mystery of Meditation

What is meditation?

Meditation is not an Indian method; it is not simply a technique. You cannot learn it. It is a growth: a growth of your total living, *out* of your total living. Meditation is not something that can be added to you as you are. It can come to you only through a basic transformation, a mutation. It is a flowering, a growth. Growth is always out of the total; it is not an addition. You must grow toward meditation.

This total flowering of the personality must be understood correctly. Otherwise one can play games with oneself, one can occupy oneself with mental tricks. And there are so many tricks! Not only can you be fooled by them, not only will you not gain anything, but in a real sense you will be harmed. The very attitude that there is some trick to meditation—to conceive of meditation in terms of method—is basically wrong. And when one begins to play with mental tricks, the very quality of the mind begins to deteriorate.

As mind exists, it is not meditative. The total mind must change before meditation can happen. Then what is the mind as it now exists? How does it function?

The mind is always verbalizing. You can know words, you can know language, you can know the conceptual structure of thinking, but that is not thinking. On the contrary, it is an escape from thinking. You see a flower and you verbalize it; you see a man crossing the street and you verbalize it. The mind can transform every existential thing into words. Then the words become a barrier, an imprisonment. This constant transformation of things into words, of existence into words, is the obstacle to a meditative mind.

So the first requirement toward a meditative mind is to be aware of your constant verbalizing and to be able to stop it. Just *see* things; do not verbalize. Be aware of their presence, but do not change them into words. Let things be, without language; let persons be, without language; let situations be, without language. It is not impossible; it is natural. It is the situation as it now exists that is artificial, but we have become so habituated to it, it has become so mechanical, that we are not even aware that we are constantly transforming experience into words.

The sunrise is there. You are never aware of the gap between seeing it and verbalizing. You see the sun, you feel it, and immediately you verbalize it. The gap between seeing and verbalizing is lost. One must become aware of the fact that the sunrise is not a word. It is a fact, a presence. The mind automatically changes experiences into words. These words then come between you and the experience.

Meditation means living without words, living nonlinguistically. Sometimes it happens spontaneously. When you are in love, presence is felt not language. Whenever two lovers are intimate with one another they become silent. It is not that there is nothing to express. On the contrary, there is an overwhelming amount to be expressed. But words are never there; they cannot be. They come only when love has gone.

If two lovers are never silent, it is an indication that love has died. Now they are filling the gap with words. When love is alive, words are not there because the very existence of love is so overwhelming, so penetrating, that the barrier of language and words is crossed. And ordinarily, it is only crossed in love.

Meditation is the culmination of love: love not for a single person, but for the total existence. To me, meditation is a living relationship with the total existence that surrounds you. If you can be in love with any situation, then you are in meditation.

And this is not a mental trick. It is not a method of stilling the mind. Rather, it requires a deep understanding of the mechanism of the mind. The moment you understand your mechanical habit of verbalization, of changing existence into words, a gap is created. It comes spontaneously. It follows understanding like a shadow.

The real problem is not how to be in meditation, but to know why you are *not* in meditation. The very process of meditation is negative. It is not adding something to you; it is negating something that has already been added.

Society cannot exist without language; it needs language. But existence does not need it. I am not saying that you should exist without language. You will have to use it. But you must be able to turn the mechanism of verbalization on and off. When you are existing as a social being, the mechanism of language is needed; but when you are alone with existence, you must be able to turn it off. If you can't turn it off—if it goes on and on, and you are incapable of stopping it—then you have become a slave to it. Mind must be an instrument, not the master.

When mind is the master, a nonmeditative state exists. When you are the master, your consciousness is the master, a meditative state exists. So meditation means becoming a master of mechanism of the mind.

Mind, and the linguistic functioning of the mind, is not the ultimate. You are beyond it; existence is beyond it. Consciousness is beyond linguistics; existence is beyond linguistics. When consciousness and existence are one, they are in communion. This communion is meditation.

Language must be dropped. I don't mean that you have to suppress it or eliminate it. I only mean that it does not have to be a twenty-four-hour-a-day habit for you. When you walk, you need to move your legs. But if they go on moving while you are sitting, then you are mad. You must be able to turn them off. In the same way, when you are not talking with anyone, language must not be there. It is a technique to communicate. When you are not communicating with anybody it should not be there.

If you are able to do this, you can grow into meditation. Meditation is a growing process, not a technique. A technique is always dead, so it can be added to you, but a process is always alive. It grows, it expands.

Language is needed, but you must not always remain in it. There must be moments when there is no verbalizing, when you just exist. It is not that you are just vegetating. Consciousness is there. And it is more acute, more alive, because language dulls it. Language is bound to be repetitive so it creates boredom. The more important language is to you, the more bored you will be.

Existence is never repetitive. Every rose is a new rose, altogether new. It has never been and it will never be again. But when we call it a rose, the word "rose" is a repetition. It has always been there; it will always be there. You have killed the new with an old word.

Existence is always young, and language is always old. Through language you escape existence, you escape life, because language is dead. The more involved you are with language, the more deadened you will be by it. A pundit is completely dead because he is nothing but language, words.

Sartre has called his autobiography *Words*. We live in words. That is, we don't live. In the end there is only a series of accumulated words and nothing else. Words are like photographs. You see something that is alive and you take a picture of it. The picture is dead. Then you make an album of dead pictures. A person who has not lived in meditation is like a dead album. Only verbal pictures are there, only memories. Nothing has been lived; everything has just been verbalized.

Meditation means living totally, but you can live totally only when you are silent. By being silent I do not mean unconscious. You can be silent and unconscious but it is not a living silence. Again, you have missed.

Through *mantras* you can autohypnotize yourself. By simply repeating a word you can create so much boredom in the mind that the mind will go to sleep. You drop into sleep, drop into the unconscious. If you go on chanting "Ram-Ram-Ram" the mind will fall asleep. Then the barrier of language is not there, but you are unconscious.

Meditation means that language must not be there, but you must be conscious. Otherwise there is no communion with existence, with all that is. No *mantra* can help, no chanting can help. Autohypnosis is not meditation. On the contrary, to be in an autohypnotic state is a regression. It is not going beyond language; it is falling below it.

So drop all *mantras*, drop all these techniques. Allow moments to exist where words are not there. You cannot get rid of words with a *mantra* because the very process uses words. You cannot eliminate language with words; it is impossible.

So what is to be done? In fact, you cannot do anything at all except to understand. Whatever you are able to do can only come from where you are. You are confused, you are not in meditation, your mind is not silent, so anything that comes out of you will only create more confusion. All that can be done right now is to begin to be aware of how the mind functions. That's all—just be aware. Awareness has nothing to do with words. It is an existential act, not a mental act.

So the first thing is to be aware. Be aware of your mental processes, how your mind works. The moment you become aware of the functioning of your mind, you are not the mind. The very awareness means that you are beyond: aloof, a witness. And the more aware you become, the more you will be able to see the gaps between the experience and the words. Gaps are there, but you are so unaware that they are never seen.

Between two words there is always a gap, however imperceptible, however small. Otherwise the two words cannot remain two; they will become one. Between two notes of music there is always a gap, a silence. Two words or two notes cannot be two unless there is an interval between them. A silence is always there but one has to be really aware, really attentive, to feel it.

The more aware you become, the slower the mind becomes. It is always relative. The less aware you are, the faster the mind is; and the more aware you are, the slower the process of the mind is. When you are more aware of the mind, the mind slows down and the gaps between thoughts widen. Then you can see them.

It is just like a film. When a projector is run in slow motion, you see the gaps. If I raise my hand, this has to be shot in a thousand parts. Each part will be a single photograph. If these thousands of single photographs pass before your eyes so fast that you cannot see the gaps, then you see the hand raised *as a process*. But in slow motion, the gaps can be seen.

Mind is just like a film. Gaps are there. The more attentive you are to your mind, the more you will see them. It is just like a gestalt picture: a picture that contains two distinct images at the same time. One image can be seen or the other can be seen, but you cannot see both simultaneously. It can be a picture of an old lady, and at the same time a picture of a young lady. But if you are focused on one, you will not see the other; and when you are focused on the other, the first is lost. Even if you know perfectly well that you have seen both images, you cannot see them simultaneously.

The same thing happens with the mind. If you see the words you cannot see the gaps, and if you see the gaps you cannot see the words. Every word is followed by a gap and every gap is followed by a word, but you cannot see both simultaneously. If you are focused on the gaps, words will be lost and you will be thrown into meditation.

A consciousness that is focused only on words is nonmeditative and a consciousness that is focused only on gaps is meditative. Whenever you become aware of the gaps, the words will be lost. If you observe carefully, you will not find words; you will only find a gap.

You can feel the difference between two words, but you cannot feel the difference between two gaps. Words are always plural and the gap is always singular: "the" gap. They merge and become one. Meditation is a focusing on the gap. Then the whole gestalt changes.

Another thing is to be understood. If you are looking at the gestalt picture and your concentration is focused on the old lady, you cannot see the other picture. But if you continue to concentrate on the old lady—if you go on focusing on her, if you become totally attentive to her—a moment will come when the focus changes and suddenly the old lady has disappeared and the other picture is there.

Why does this happen? It happens because the mind cannot be focused continuously for a long time. It has to change or it will go to sleep. These are the only two possibilities. If you go on concentrating on one thing, the mind will fall asleep. It cannot remain fixed; it is a living process. If you let it become bored it will go to sleep in order to escape from the stagnancy of your focus. Then it can continue living, in dreams.

This is meditation Mahesh Yogi-style. It's peaceful, refreshing, it can help your physical health and mental equilibrium, but it is not meditation. The same thing can be done by autohypnosis. The Indian word *mantra* means suggestion, nothing else. To take this as meditation is a serious mistake. It is not. And if you think of it as meditation, you will never search for authentic meditation. That is the real harm that is done by such practices and propagandists of such practices. It is just drugging yourself psychologically.

So don't use any *mantra* to push words out of the way. Just become aware of the words and the focus of your mind will change automatically to the gaps.

If you identify with words, you will go on jumping from one word to another and you will miss the gap. Another word is something new to focus on. The mind goes on changing; the focus changes. But if you are not identified with words, if you are just a witness—aloof, just watching the words as they go by in a procession—then the whole focus will change and you will become aware of the gap. It is just as if you are on the street, watching people as they pass by. One person has passed and another has not yet come. There is a gap; the street is vacant. If you are watching, then you will know the gap.

And once you know the gap, you are in it; you have jumped into it. It is an abyss—so peace-giving, so consciousness-creating. It is meditation to be in the gap; it is transformation. Now language is not needed; you will drop it. It is a conscious dropping. You are conscious of the silence, the infinite silence. You are part of it, one with it. You are not conscious of the abyss as the other; you are conscious of the abyss as yourself. You *know*, but now you are the knowing. You observe the gap, but now the observer is the observed.

As far as words and thoughts are concerned, you are a witness, separate, and words are the other. But when there are no words, you are the gap—yet still conscious that you are. Between you and the gap, between consciousness and existence, there is no barrier now. Only words are the barrier. Now you are in an existential situation. This is meditation: to be one with existence; to be totally in it and still conscious. This is the contradiction, this is the paradox. Now you have known a situation in which you were conscious, and yet one with it.

Ordinarily, when we are conscious of anything, the thing becomes the other. If we are identified with something, then it is not the other, but then we are not conscious (as in anger, in sex). We become one only when we are unconscious.

Sex has so much appeal because in sex you become one for a moment. But in that moment, you are unconscious. You seek the unconsciousness because you seek the oneness. But the more you seek it, the more conscious you become. Then you will not feel the bliss of sex, because the bliss was coming from the unconsciousness.

You could become unconscious in a moment of passion. Your consciousness dropped. For a single moment you were in the abyss—but unconscious. But the more you seek it, the more it is lost. Finally a moment comes when you are in sex and the moment of unconsciousness no longer happens. The abyss is lost, the bliss is lost. Then the act becomes stupid. It is just a mechanical release; there is nothing spiritual about it.

We have known only unconscious oneness; we have never known conscious oneness. Meditation is conscious oneness. It is the other pole of sexuality. Sex is one pole (unconscious oneness) and meditation is the other pole (conscious oneness). Sex is the lowest point of oneness and meditation is the peak, the highest peak of oneness. The difference is a difference of consciousness.

The Western mind is thinking about meditation now because the appeal of sex has been lost. Whenever a society becomes non-suppressive sexually, meditation will follow, because uninhibited sex will kill the charm and romance of sex; it will kill the spiritual side of it. Much sex is there, but you cannot continue to be unconscious in it.

A sexually suppressed society can remain sexual, but a non-suppressive, uninhibited society cannot remain with sexuality forever. It will have to be transcended. So if a society is sexual, meditation will follow. To me, a sexuality free society is the first step toward seeking, searching.

But of course, because the search is there, it can be exploited. It is being exploited by the East. Gurus can be supplied; they can be exported. And they *are* being exported. But only tricks can be learned through these gurus. Understanding comes through life, through living. It cannot be given, transferred.

I cannot give you my understanding. I can talk about it, but I cannot give it to you. You will have to find it. You will have to go into life. You will have to err; you will have to fail; you will have to pass through many frustrations. But only through failures, errors, frustrations, only through the encounter of real living, will you come to meditation. That is why I say it is a growth.

Something can be understood, but understanding that comes through another can never be more than intellectual. That is why

Krishnamurti demands the impossible. He says, "Do not understand me intellectually"—but nothing except intellectual understanding can come from someone else. That is why Krishnamurti's effort has been absurd. What he is saying is authentic, but when he demands more than intellectual understanding from the listener it is impossible. Nothing more can come from someone else, nothing more can be delivered.

But intellectual understanding can be enough. If you can understand what I am saying intellectually, you can also understand what has *not* been said. You can also understand the gaps: what I am not saying, what I *cannot* say. The first understanding is bound to be intellectual, because the intellect is the door. It can never be spiritual. Spirituality is the inner shrine.

I can only communicate to you intellectually. If you can really understand it, then what has not been said can be felt. I cannot communicate without words, but when I am using words I am also using silences. You will have to be aware of both. If only words are being understood then it is a communication; but if you can be aware of the gaps also, then it is a communion.

One has to begin somewhere. Every beginning is bound to be a false beginning, but one has to begin. Through the false, through the groping, the door is found. One who thinks that he will begin only when the right beginning is there will never begin at all. Even a false step is a step in the right direction because it is a *step*, a beginning. You begin to grope in the dark and, through groping, the door is found.

That is why I said to be aware of the linguistic process—the process of words—and to seek an awareness of the gaps, the intervals. There will be moments when there will be no conscious effort on your part and you will become aware of the gaps. That is the encounter with the divine, the encounter with the existential.

Whenever there is an encounter, do not escape from it. Be with it. It will be fearful at first; it is bound to be. Whenever the unknown is encountered, fear is created because to us the unknown is death. So whenever there is a gap, you will feel death coming to you. Then be dead! Just be in it, and die completely in the gap. And you will be resurrected. By dying your death in silence, life is resurrected. You are alive for the first time, really alive.

So to me, meditation is not a method but a process; meditation is not a technique but an understanding. It cannot be taught; it can only be indicated. You cannot be informed about it because no information is really information. It is from the outside, and meditation comes from your own inner depths.

So search, be a seeker, and do not be a disciple. Then you will not be a disciple of some guru, but a disciple of the total life. Then you will not just be learning words. Spiritual learning cannot come from words but from the gaps, the silences that are always surrounding you. They are there even in the crowd, in the market, in the bazaar. Seek the silences, seek the gaps within and without, and one day you will find that you are in meditation.

Meditation comes to you. It always comes; you cannot bring it. But one has to be in search of it, because only when you are in search will you be open to it, vulnerable to it. You are a host to it. Meditation is a guest. You can invite it and wait for it. It comes to Buddha, it comes to Jesus, it comes to everybody who is ready, who is open and seeking.

But do not learn it from somewhere; otherwise you will be tricked. The mind is always searching for something easier. This becomes the source for exploitation. Then there are gurus and gurudoms, and spiritual life is poisoned.

The most dangerous person is the one who exploits someone's spiritual urge. If someone robs you of your wealth it is not so serious, if someone fails you it is not so serious, but if someone tricks you and kills, or even postpones, your urge toward meditation, toward the divine, toward ecstasy, then the sin is great and unforgivable.

But that is being done. So be aware of it, and don't ask anybody, "What is meditation? How do I meditate?" Instead, ask what the hindrances are, what the obstacles are. Ask why we aren't always in meditation, where the growth has been stopped, where we have been crippled. And do not seek a guru because gurus are crippling. Anyone who gives you ready-made formulas is not a friend but an enemy.

Grope in the dark. Nothing else can be done. The very groping will become the understanding that will liberate you from darkness. Jesus said: "Truth is freedom." Understand this freedom. Truth is always through understanding. It is not something that you meet and encounter; it is something you grow into. So be in search of understanding, because the more understanding you become, the nearer you will be to truth. And in some unknown, unexpected, unpredictable moment, when understanding comes to a peak, you are in the abyss. You are no more, and meditation is.

When you are no more, you are in meditation. Meditation is not *more* of you; it is always *beyond* you. When you are in the abyss, meditation is there. Then the ego is not; then you are not. Then the being is. That is what religions mean by God: the ultimate being. It is the essence of all religions, all searches, but it is not to be found anywhere ready-made. So be aware of anyone who makes claims about it.

Go on groping and don't be afraid of failure. Admit failures, but do not commit the same failures again. Once is all; that is enough. The person who goes on erring in the search for truth is always forgiven. It is a promise from the very depths of existence.

3

Sex, Love and Prayer: Three Steps to the Divine

Please describe to us the spiritual significance of sex energy. How can we sublimate and spiritualize sex? Is it possible to have sex, to make love, as a meditation, as a jumping board toward higher levels of consciousness?

There is no such thing as sex energy. Energy is one and the same. Sex is one outlet for it, one direction for it; it is one of the applications of the energy. Life energy is one, but it can manifest in many directions. Sex is one of them. When life energy becomes biological, it becomes sex energy.

Sex is just an application of the life energy. So there is no question of sublimation. If life energy flows in another direction, there is no sex. But it is not a sublimation; it is a transformation.

Sex is the natural, biological flow of life energy, and the lowest application of it. It is natural because life cannot exist without it, and the lowest because it is the foundation not the peak. When sex becomes the totality, the whole life is just a waste. It is like laying a foundation and going on laying the foundation, without ever building the house for which the foundation is meant.

Sex is just an opportunity for a higher transformation of life energy. As far as it goes it is all right, but when sex becomes the whole, when it becomes the sole outlet for life energy, then it becomes destructive. It can only be the means not the end. And means are meaningful only when the ends are achieved. When a man abuses the means, the whole purpose is destroyed. If sex becomes the center of life (as it has become), then means are changed into ends. Sex creates the biological foundation for life to exist, to continue. It is a means; it should not become the end.

The moment sex becomes the end, the spiritual dimension is lost. But if sex becomes meditative, then it is directed toward the spiritual dimension. It becomes a stepping stone, a jumping board.

There is no need for sublimation, because energy as such is neither sexual nor spiritual. Energy is always neutral. In itself, it is nameless. The name comes from the door through which it flows. The name is not the name of the energy itself; it is the name of the form that the energy takes. When you say "sexual energy," it means energy that flows through a sexual outlet, through a biological outlet. This same energy is spiritual energy when it flows into the divine.

Energy itself is neutral. When it is expressed biologically, it is sex. When it is expressed emotionally, it may become love, it may become hate, it may become anger. When it is expressed intellectually, it may become scientific, it may become literary. When it moves through the body, it becomes physical. When it moves through the mind, it becomes mental. The differences are not differences of energy as such, but of the applied manifestations of it.

So it is not right to say "sublimation of sex energy." If the outlet of sex is not used, the energy becomes pure again. Energy is always pure. When it is manifested through the divine door it becomes spiritual, but the form is just a manifestation of the energy.

The word "sublimation" has very bad associations. All theories of sublimation are theories of suppression. Whenever you say "sublimation of sex," you have become antagonistic to it. Your condemnation is there in the very word.

You ask what one can do about sex. Anything done directly to sex is a suppression. There are only indirect methods in which you do not concern yourself with sexual energy at all but, rather, seek to open the door to the divine. When the gate to the divine is open, all the energies that are within you begin to flow toward that door. Sex is absorbed. Whenever a higher bliss is possible, the lower forms of bliss become irrelevant. You are not to suppress them or fight against them. They just wither away. Sex is not sublimated; it is transcended.

Anything done negatively with sex will not transform the energy. On the contrary, it will create a conflict within you that will be destructive. When you fight with an energy, you are fighting with yourself. No one can win the fight. One moment you will feel that you have won, and the next moment you will feel that sex has won. This will go on continuously. Sometimes there will be no sex and you will feel that you have controlled it, and the next moment you will feel the pull of sex again and everything you seem to have gained will be lost. No one can win a fight against his own energy.

If your energies are needed somewhere else, somewhere more blissful, sex will disappear. It is not that the energy is sublimated; it is not that you have done something to it. Rather, a new way toward greater bliss has opened for you and automatically, spontaneously, the energy begins to flow toward the new door.

If you are holding stones and suddenly diamonds come your way, you will never even notice that you drop the stones. They will drop by themselves, as if you never had them. You won't even remember your renunciation of them, that you have thrown them away. You won't even realize it. It is not that something has been sublimated. A greater source of happiness has been opened, and the lesser sources have dropped away by themselves.

This is so automatic, so spontaneous, that no positive action against sex is needed. Whenever you are doing anything against any energy it is negative. The real, positive action is not even connected with sex but is concerned with meditation. You will not even know that sex has gone. It has simply been absorbed by the new.

Sublimation is an ugly word. It carries a tone of antagonism, of conflict, in it. Sex should be taken for what it is. It is just the biological foundation for life to exist. Do not give it any spiritual or antispiritual meaning. Simply understand the fact of it.

When you take it as a biological fact, then you are not concerned with it at all. You become concerned with it only when some spiritual meaning is given to it. So do not give any meaning to it; do not create any philosophy around it. Just see the facts. Do not do anything for it or against it. Let it be as it is; accept it as normal. Don't take an abnormal attitude toward it.

Just as you have eyes and hands, so too you have sex. You are not against your eyes or your hands, so do not be against sex. Then the question of what to do about sex becomes irrelevant. To create a dichotomy for or against sex is meaningless. It is a given fact. You have come into existence through sex, and you have a built-in program to give birth through sex again. You are part of a great continuity. Your body is going to die, so it has a built-in program to create another body to replace it.

Death is certain. That is why sex is so obsessive. You will not be here forever, so you will have to be replaced by a newer body, a replica. Sex is so important, because the whole nature insists on it; otherwise man could not continue to be. If it were voluntary, there would be no one left on earth. Sex is so obsessive, so compelling, the sex drive is so intense, because the whole of nature is for it. Without it, life cannot exist.

The reason why sex is so important to religious seekers is because it is so nonvoluntary, so compelling, so natural. It has become a criterion to know whether the life energy in a particular person has reached the divine. We cannot know directly that someone has encountered the divine—we cannot know directly that someone has diamonds—but we can know directly whether someone has thrown the stones, because we are acquainted with stones. We can know directly that someone has transcended sex because we are acquainted with sex.

Sex is so compulsive, so nonvoluntary, it is so great a force, that it cannot be transcended until someone has achieved the divine. So *bramacharya* became a criterion to know whether a person has reached the divine. Then sex, as it exists in normal beings, will not exist for him.

This does not mean that by dropping sex one will achieve the divine. The reverse is a fallacy. The person who has found diamonds throws the stones he was carrying, but the reverse of this is not true. You can throw away the stones, but that doesn't mean you have achieved something beyond it.

Then you will be in between. You will have a suppressed mind, not a transcended one. Sex will go on bubbling inside you and will create an inner hell. This is not going beyond sex. When sex becomes suppressed it becomes ugly, diseased, neurotic. It becomes perverted.

The so-called religious attitude toward sex has created a perverted sexuality, a culture that is completely neurotic sexually. I am not in favor of it. Sex is a biological fact; there is nothing wrong in it. So do not fight it or it will become perverted, and a perverted sex is not a step forward. It is falling below normality;

it is a step toward insanity. When the suppression becomes so intense that you cannot prolong it, then it explodes—and in that explosion, you will be lost.

You are *all* human qualities, you are *all* possibilities. The normal fact of sex is healthy, but when it becomes abnormally suppressed it becomes unhealthy. You can move toward the divine from the normal very easily, but to move to the divine from a neurotic mind becomes arduous and, in a way, impossible. First you will have to become healthy, normal. Then, in the end, there is a possibility that sex may be transcended.

Then what is to be done? Know sex! Move into it consciously! This is the secret to open up a new door. If you go into sex unconsciously, then you are just an instrument in the hands of biological evolution; but if you can be conscious in the sex act, the very consciousness becomes a deep meditation.

The sex act is so involuntary and so compulsive that it is difficult to be conscious in it, but it is not impossible. And if you can be conscious in the sex act, then there is no other act in life in which you cannot be conscious, because no act is as deep as sex.

If you can become aware in the sex act, then even in death you will be aware. The depth of the sex act and the depth of death are the same, parallel. You come to the same point. So if you can be aware in the sex act you have achieved a great thing. It is invaluable.

So use sex as an act of meditation. Do not fight it, do not go against it. You cannot fight with nature; you are part and parcel of it. You must have a friendly, sympathetic attitude toward sex. It is the deepest dialogue between you and nature.

In fact, the sex act is not really a dialogue between a man and a woman. It is a dialogue of man with nature, through woman; and of woman with nature, through man. It is a dialogue with nature. For a moment you are in the cosmic flow; you are in the celestial harmony; you are in tune with the whole. In this way, man is fulfilled through woman and woman through man.

Man is not whole and woman is not whole. They are two fragments of one whole. So whenever they become one in the sexual act, they can be in harmony with the innermost nature of things, with the Tao. This harmony can be a biological birth for a new being. If you are unaware, that is the only possibility. But if you are aware, the act can become a birth for *you*, a spiritual birth. You will be "twice-born" through it.

The moment you participate in it consciously, you become a witness to it. And once you can become a witness in the sex act you will transcend sex, because in witnessing you become free. Now the compulsion will not be there. You will not be an unconscious participant. Once you have become a witness in the act, you have transcended it. Now you know that you are not the body alone. The witnessing force in you has known something beyond it.

This "beyond" can be known only when you are deeply within. It is not a surface encounter. When you are bargaining in the market, your consciousness cannot go very deep because the act itself is superficial. As far as man is concerned, the sex act is ordinarily the only act through which one can become a witness to the inner depths.

The more you go into meditation through sex, the less effect sex will have. Meditation will grow from it, and out of the growing meditation a new door will open and sex will wither away. It will not be a sublimation. It will be just like dry leaves falling from a tree. The tree never even knows the leaves are falling. In the same way, you will never even know that the mechanical urge for sex is going.

Create meditation out of sex; make sex an object of meditation.* Treat it as a temple and you will transcend it and be transformed. Then sex will not be there, but there will not be any suppression, any sublimation. Sex will just become irrelevant, meaningless. You have grown beyond it. It makes no sense to you now.

It is just like a child growing up. Now toys are meaningless. He has not sublimated anything; he has not suppressed anything. He has just grown up; he has become mature. Toys are meaningless now. They are childish and now the child is no longer a child.

In the same way, the more you meditate, the less sex will have an appeal to you. And by and by, spontaneously, without a con-

* A wide variety of meditation techniques that work directly with sex energy are discussed by Bhagwan in a series of eighty lectures on the *Vigyana Bhairava Tantra*. See *The Book of the Secrets* (volume 1, Harper & Row, 10 East 53d Street, New York; volumes 2-5, Rajneesh Foundation, 17 Koregaon Park, Poona, India).

scious effort to sublimate sex, energy will have a new source to flow to. The same energy that has flowed through sex will now flow through meditation. And when it flows through meditation, the divine door is being opened.

Another thing. You have used the words "sex" and "love." Ordinarily we use both words as if they have an inner association. They have not. Love comes only when sex has gone. Before that, love is just a lure, a foreplay, and nothing else. It is just preparing the ground for the sex act. It is nothing but an introduction to sex, a preface. So the more sex there is between two persons, the less love there will be because then the preface is not needed.

If two persons are in love, and if there is no sex between them, there will be much romantic love. But the moment sex comes in, love goes out. Sex is so abrupt. In itself, it is so violent. It needs an introduction; it needs foreplay. Love, as we know it, is just clothing for the naked fact of sex. If you look deeply into what you call love you will find sex standing there, preparing to jump. It is always around the corner. Love is talking. Sex is preparing.

This so-called love is associated with sex, but only as a preface. If sex comes, then the love will drop. That's why marriage kills romantic love, and kills it absolutely. The two persons become acquainted with each other and the foreplay, the love, becomes unnecessary.

Real love is not a preface. It is a fragrance. It is not before sex, but after. It is not a prologue but an epilogue. If you have passed through sex and feel compassion for the other, then love develops. And if you meditate, you will feel compassionate. If you meditate in the sex act, then your sexual partner will not be just an instrument for your physical pleasure. You will feel gratitude to him or her because you have both come to a deep meditation.

When you meditate in sex, a new friendliness will arise between the two of you because, through each other, you have come into communion with nature; through each other, you have had a glimpse into the unknown depths of reality. You will feel grateful and compassionate to each other: compassion for the suffering; compassion for the search; compassion for a fellow being, a fellow traveler; compassion for a groping friend.

If sex becomes meditative, only then is there a fragrance that lingers behind: a feeling that is not a foreplay of sex but a maturity, a growth, a meditative realization. So if the sex act becomes meditative, you will feel love. Love is a combination of gratefulness, friendliness and compassion. If these three are there, then you are in love.

If this love develops, it will transcend sex. Love develops *through* sex, but goes beyond it. Just like a flower: it comes through the roots, but goes beyond. And it will not come back; there is no reversal. So if love develops, no sex will be there. In fact, that is one of the ways of knowing that love has developed. Sex is like the shell of an egg, a shell through which love has to emerge. The moment it emerges, the shell will no longer be there. It will be broken, discarded.

Sex can reach love only when meditation is there; otherwise not. If meditation is not there, the same sex will be repeated and you will become bored. Sex will become increasingly dull, and you will not feel grateful to the other. Rather, you will feel cheated; you will feel inimical to him. He dominates you. He dominates through sex, because it has become a need for you. You have become a slave because you cannot live without sex. But you can never feel friendly toward one to whom you have become a slave.

And both feel the same: that the other is the master. The domination will be denied and fought, but sex will still be repeated. It will become a daily routine. You fight with your sex partner, and then make things right again. Then again you fight; then again you make up. Love is just an adjustment at the most. You cannot feel friendly; there is no compassion. Instead there will be cruelty and violence; you will feel cheated. You have become a slave. Sex will not be able to develop into love. It will remain just sex.

Go through sex! Do not be afraid of it, because fear leads nowhere. If one has to be afraid of anything, it is only of fear itself. Do not fear sex and do not fight it because that too is a sort of fear. "Fight or flight"—fight or escape—these are two paths of fear. So do not escape sex; do not fight it. Accept it; take it for granted. Go deep in it, know it totally, understand it, meditate in it and you will transcend it. The minute you meditate in the sex act, a new door is opened. You come upon a new dimension, a very unknown, unheard-of one, and greater bliss flows through.

You will encounter something so blissful that sex will become irrelevant and it will subside by itself. Now your energy will no longer flow in that direction. Energy always flows toward bliss. Because bliss appears in sex, energy flows toward it, but if you seek more bliss—a bliss that transcends sex, that goes beyond sex, a bliss that is more fulfilling, deeper, greater—then, by itself, energy will stop flowing toward sex.

When sex becomes a meditation it flowers into love, and this flowering is a movement toward the divine. That is why love is divine. Sex is physical; love is spiritual. And if the flower of love is there, prayer will come; it will follow. Now you are not far from the divine. You are near home.

Now, begin to meditate on love. This is the second step. When the moment of communion is there, when the moment of love is there, begin to meditate. Go deep in it; be aware of it. Now bodies are not meeting. In sex, bodies were meeting; in love, souls are meeting. It is still a meeting, a meeting between two persons.

Now, see love as you have seen sex. See the communion, the inner meeting, the inner intercourse. Then you will transcend even love, and you will come to prayer. This prayer is the door. It is still a meeting, but not a meeting between two persons. It is a communion between you and the whole. Now the other, as a person, is dropped. It is the impersonal other—the whole existence —and you.

But prayer is still a meeting, so ultimately it also has to be transcended. In prayer, the devotee and the divine are different; the *bhakta* and the *bhagwan* are different. It is still a meeting. That is why Meera, or Theresa, could use sexual terms for their prayer experiences.

One must meditate in prayerful moments. Again, be a witness to it. See the communion between you and the whole. This requires the subtlest awareness possible. If you can be aware of the meeting between you and the whole, then you transcend yourself and the whole, both. Then you *are* the whole. And in this whole, there is no duality; there is only oneness.

This oneness is sought through sex, through love, through prayer. This oneness is what is longed for. Even in sex, the longing is for the oneness. Bliss comes because, for a single moment, you have become one. Sex deepens into love, love deepens into prayer, and prayer deepens into a total transcendence, a total oneness.

This deepening is always through meditation. The method is always the same. Levels differ, dimensions differ, steps differ, but the method is the same. Dig into sex and you will find love. Go deep into love and you will come to prayer. Dig into prayer and you will explode into oneness. This oneness is the total, this oneness is the bliss, this oneness is the ecstasy.

So it is essential not to take a fighting attitude. In every fact, the divine is present. It may be garbed, it may be clothed, but you must strip it, unclothe it. You will find still more subtle garbs. Again, undress it. Unless you encounter the oneness in its total nakedness, you will not find satisfaction; you will not feel fulfilled.

The moment you come to the ungarbed *one*, the unclothed *one*, you become one with it, because when you know the naked, it is no one but you. In fact, everyone is searching for himself through others. One has to find one's own home by knocking on others' doors.

The moment reality is disrobed you are one with it, because the difference is only of garbs. Clothes are the barrier, so you cannot disrobe reality unless you disrobe yourself. That is why meditation is a double weapon: it disrobes reality and it disrobes you as well. The reality becomes naked, and you become naked. And in a moment of total nakedness, total emptiness, you become the *one*.

So I am not against sex. That doesn't mean I am *for* sex. It means that I am for going deep in it and uncovering the beyond. The beyond is always there, but ordinary sex is hit-and-run sex, so no one goes deep. If you can go deep, you will feel grateful to the divine that, through sex, a door is opened; but if sex is just hit-and-run, you will never know that you were close to something greater.

We are so cunning that we have created a false love that does not come after sex but before it. It is a cultivated, artificial thing. That's why we feel that love is lost when sex is fulfilled. Love was just the preface, and now the preface is no longer needed. But real love is always beyond sex; it is hiding behind sex. Go deep in it, meditate in it religiously, and you will flower into a loving state of mind.

I am not against sex and I am not *for* love. You still have to transcend it. Meditate on it; transcend it. By *meditation* I mean you have to pass through it fully alert, aware. You must not pass through it blindly, unconsciously. Great bliss is there, but you can pass by blindly and miss it. This blindness has to be transformed; you must become open-eyed. With open eyes, sex can take you on the path of oneness.

The drop can become the ocean. That is the longing within every drop's heart. In every act, in every desire, you will find the same longing. Uncover it, follow it. It is a great adventure! As we live our lives today, we are unconscious. But this much can be done. It is arduous, but it is not impossible. It has been possible for a Jesus, for a Buddha, for a Mahavir, and it is possible for everyone else.

When you go into sex with this intensity, with this alertness, with this sensitivity, you will transcend it. There will not be any sublimation at all. When you transcend, there will be no sex, not even sublimated sex. There will be love, prayer, and oneness.

These are the three stages of love: physical love, psychic love and spiritual love. And when these three are transcended, there is the divine. When Jesus said, "God is love," this was the closest definition possible, because the last thing we know on the path toward God is love. Beyond that is the unknown, and the unknown cannot be defined. We can only indicate the divine through our last realization: love. Beyond that point of love, there is no experience because there is no experiencer. The drop has become the ocean!

Go step by step, but with a friendly attitude. With no tension, no struggle. Just go with alertness. Alertness is the only light in the dark night of life. With this light, go into it. Seek and search every corner. Everywhere is the divine, so do not be against anything.

But do not remain with anything either. Go beyond, because still greater bliss awaits you. The journey must continue. If you are near sex, use sex. If you are near love, use love. Do not think in terms of suppression or sublimation; do not think in terms of fighting. The divine may be hiding behind anything, so do not fight; do not escape from anything. In fact, it *is* behind everything, so wherever you are, take the closest door and you will progress. Do not become stagnant anywhere and you will reach, because life is everywhere.

Jesus said, "Under every stone is the Lord," but you see only the stones. You will have to pass through this stony state of mind. When you see sex as an enemy, it becomes a stone. Then it becomes nontransparent; you cannot see beyond it. Use it, meditate on it, and the stone will become just like glass. You will see behind it, and you will forget the glass. What is behind the glass will be remembered.

Anything that becomes transparent will disappear. So do not make sex a stone; make it transparent. And it becomes transparent through meditation.

4

Kundalini Yoga: Returning to the Roots

What is kundalini yoga and how can it help the West? Why is your method for awakening kundalini chaotic rather than like the traditional, controlled methods?

Existence is energy, the movement of energy in so many ways and so many forms. As far as human existence is concerned, this energy is kundalini energy. Kundalini is the focused energy of the human body and human psyche.

Energy can exist either manifested or unmanifested. It can remain in the seed, or it can come up in a manifested form. Every energy is either in the seed or in the manifested form. Kundalini means your total potential, your total possibility. But it is a seed; it is the potential. The ways to awaken kundalini are ways to make your potential actual.

So first of all, kundalini is not something unique. It is only human energy as such. But ordinarily only a part of it is functioning, a very minute part. And even that part is not functioning harmoniously; it is in conflict. That is the misery, the anguish. If your energy can function harmoniously then you feel bliss, but if it is in conflict—if it is antagonistic to itself—then you feel miserable. All misery means that your energy is in conflict, and all happiness, all bliss, means that your energy is in harmony.

Why is the whole energy only potential, not actual? Because, it is not needed as far as day-to-day life is concerned; it is not required. Only that part becomes functional that is required, challenged. Day-to-day life is not a challenge to it, so only a very minute part becomes manifest. And even this small, manifested part is not harmonious because your day-to-day life is not integrated.

Your needs are in conflict. Society requires one thing and your instincts require something quite contradictory. Social requirements and personal requirements are in conflict. Society has its requirements; morality and religion have their requirements. These conflicts have prevented man from being a harmonious whole. They have made man fragmentary.

In the morning, one thing is required; in the afternoon, something else is required. Your wife requires something from you; your mother requires something quite contrary. Then day-to-day life becomes a conflicting demand on you, and the minute part of your total energy that has become manifest is in conflict with itself.

There is also another conflict. The part that has become manifest will always be in conflict with the part that has not yet become manifest; the actual will always be in conflict with the potential. The potential will push itself to be manifested, and the actual will suppress it.

To use psychological terms, the unconscious is always in conflict with the conscious. The conscious will try to dominate it, because it is always in danger of the unconscious manifesting itself. The conscious is under control and the potential, the unconscious, is not. You can manage the conscious, but with an explosion of the unconscious you will be in insecurity. You will not be able to manage it. That is the fear of the conscious. So this is the other conflict, greater and deeper than the first: the conflict between the conscious and the unconscious, between the energy that has become manifest and the energy that wants to be manifested.

These two types of conflict are why you are not in harmony. And if you are not in harmony, your energy will become antagonistic to you. Energy needs movement, and movement is always from the unmanifest toward the manifest, from the seed toward the tree, from the dark toward the light.

This movement is possible only if there is no suppression. Otherwise the movement, the harmony, is destroyed and your energy becomes an enemy to you. You become a house divided against itself; you become a crowd. Then you are not one; you are many.

This is the situation that exists as far as human beings are concerned. But this should not be. This is why there is ugliness and misery. Bliss and beauty can come only when your life energy is in movement, in easy movement, relaxed movement—unsuppressed, uninhibited; integrated, not fragmentary; not in conflict with itself, but one and organic. When your energy comes to this harmonious unity, that is what is meant by kundalini. Kundalini is just a technical term for your whole energy when it is in unity, in movement, in harmony, without any conflict; when it is cooperative, complementary and organic. Then and there, there is a transformation—unique and unknown.

When energies are in conflict, you want to relieve them. You feel at ease only when your conflicting energies are released, thrown off. But whenever you throw them off, your life energy, your vitality, moves downward, or outward. The downward movement is the outward movement, and the upward movement is the inward movement. The more your energies go up, the more they go in; the more they go down, the more they move out. If you throw your conflicting energies out you will feel relief, but that is just like throwing your life away in bits and fragments, in installments. It is suicidal. Unless our life energy becomes one and harmonious, and the flow becomes inward, we are suicidal.

When you are throwing out energy you feel relieved, but the relief is bound to be momentary because you are a constant source of energy. Energy accumulates again and you will have to get rid of it again. What is ordinarily known as pleasure is just a throwing off of conflicting energies. Pleasure means that you are relieved of a burden. It is always negative, never positive. But bliss is positive. It comes only when your energies are fulfilled.

When your energies are not thrown out but have an inward flowering, when you become one with them and are not in conflict with them, then there is a movement inward. That movement is endless. It becomes deeper and deeper, and the deeper it goes, the more blissful it becomes, the more ecstatic.

So energy can have two possibilities. The first is just a relief, a throwing off of energies which have become a burden to you, which you could not utilize and with which you could not be creative. This state of mind is anti-kundalini.

The ordinary state of human beings is anti-kundalini. Energy moves from the center toward the periphery because that is the direction *you* are moving toward. Kundalini means just the opposite. Forces, energies, move from the periphery toward the center.

The movement inward, the center-oriented movement, is blissful, while the outward movement gives both happiness and misery.

There will be momentary happiness and permanent misery. Happiness will come only in gaps. Only when you hope, only when you have expectations, is the gap there. The actual result is always misery.

Happiness is in expectation, in hoping, in desiring, in dreaming. It is only that you are relieved of your burden; the happiness is totally negative. There is no happiness as such, but only the momentary absence of misery. That absence is taken as happiness.

You are constantly creating new energies. That is what is meant by life: the ability to go on creating the life force. The moment the capacity is gone, you are dead. This is the paradox: you go on creating energy and you don't know what to do with it. When it is created you throw it off and when it is not created you feel miserable, ill.

The moment the life force is not created, you feel ill; but when it is created, you again feel ill. The first illness is that of weakness, and the second illness is that of energy that has become a burden to you. You are not able to harmonize it, to make it creative, to make it blissful. You have created it and now you don't know what to do with it, so you just throw it off. Then you create more energy again. This is absurd, but this absurdity is what we ordinarily mean by human existence: constantly creating energy that constantly becomes burdensome and that you constantly have to relieve.

That is why sex has become so important, so significant—because it is one of the greatest means to rid yourself of energy. If the society becomes affluent, you have more sources through which energy can be created. Then you become more sexual, because you have more tensions to relieve.

There is a constant creating of energy and throwing out of energy. If one is intelligent enough, sensitive enough, then one will feel the absurdity of it, the whole meaninglessness of it. Then one will feel the purposelessness of life. Are you just an instrument to create energy and throw it out? What is the meaning of this? What is the need to exist at all? Just to be an instrument in which energy is created and thrown out? So the more sensitive a person is, the more he feels the meaninglessness of life as we know it.

Kundalini means to change this absurd situation into a meaningful one. The science of kundalini is one of the most subtle sciences.

The physical sciences are also concerned with energy, but with material energy not psychic energy. Yoga is concerned with psychic energy. It is a science of the metaphysical, of that which is transcendental.

Just like the material energy that science is concerned with, this psychic energy can be creative or destructive. If it is not used, it becomes destructive; if it is used, it becomes creative. But it can also be used noncreatively. The way to make it creative is first to understand that you should not realize only part of your potential. If one part is realized and the remaining, major portion of your potential is unrealized, it is not a situation that can be creative.

The *whole* must be realized; your whole potential must be actualized. There are methods to realize the potential, to make it actual, to make it awake. It is sleeping, just like a snake. That is why it has been named kundalini: serpent power, a sleeping serpent.

If you have ever seen a serpent sleeping, it is just like that. It is coiled; there is no movement at all. But a serpent can stand up straight on its tail. It stands by its energy. That is why the serpent has been used symbolically. Your life energy is also coiled and asleep. But it can become straight; it can become awake, with its full potential actualized. Then you will be transformed.

Life and death are only two states of energy. Life means energy functioning, and death means energy nonfunctioning. Life means energy awake; death means energy gone again into sleep. So according to kundalini yoga, you are ordinarily only partially alive. The part of your energy that has become actualized is your life. The remaining part is so asleep that it is as if it were not.

But it can be awakened. There are so many methods through which kundalini yoga tries to make the potential actual. For example, *pranayama* (breath control) is one of the methods to hammer the sleeping energy. Through breath, the hammering is possible because breathing is the bridge between your vital energy —your *prana*, your original source of vitality—and your actual existence. It is the bridge between the potential and the actual.

The moment you change your breathing system, your total energy system changes. When you are asleep your breathing changes. When you are awake your breathing changes. When you are angry your breathing is different; when you are in love your breathing is different; when you are in sexual passion your breathing is different. In every state of mind a particular quality of life force is there, so your breathing changes.

When you are angry you require more energy on the periphery. If you are in danger—if you have to attack or you have to defend yourself—more energy is needed on the periphery. The energy will rush from the center.

Because a great quantity of energy is thrown off from your body during the sex act, you feel exhausted afterward. And after anger, too, you will feel exhausted. But after a loving moment, you will not feel exhausted. You will feel fresh. After prayer, you will feel fresh. Why has the contrary happened? When you are in a loving moment, energy is not needed on the periphery because there is no danger. You are at ease, relaxed, so the energy flow is inward. When energy flows inward, you feel fresh.

After deep breathing you will feel fresh, because energy is flowing inward. When energy flows inward you feel vitalized, fulfilled; you feel a well-being.

Another thing to notice: when energy is going inward, your breath will begin to have a different quality. It will be relaxed, rhythmic, harmonious. There will be moments when you will not feel it at all, when you will feel as if it has stopped. It becomes so subtle! Because energy is not needed, the breath stops. In *samadhi*, in ecstasy, one feels that the breath has stopped completely. No outward flow of energy is needed, so the breath is unnecessary.

Through *pranayama* this potential energy within you is systematically awakened. It can also be tapped through *asanas* (yogic postures), because your body is connected at every point to the source of energy. So every posture has a corresponding effect on the energy source.

The posture that Buddha used is called *padmasan*, the lotus posture. It is one of the postures in which the least amount of energy is needed. If you sit up straight, sitting is so balanced that you become one with the earth. There is no gravitational pull. And if your hands and feet are in such a position that a closed circuit is created, the life electricity will flow in a circuit. Buddha's posture is a round posture. Energy becomes circular; it is not thrown out.

Energy always moves out through the fingers, hands or feet.

But through a round shape, energy cannot flow out. That is why women are more resistent to illness than men, and why they live longer. The rounder the body is, the less energy flows outward.

Women are not so exhausted after the sex act because the shape of their sexual organ is round and absorbing. Men will be more exhausted. Because of the shape of their sexual organ, more energy is thrown out. Not only biological energy, but psychic energy also.

All the energy outlets are joined together in *padmasan,* so no energy can move outward. Both feet are crossed, the hands touch the feet and the feet touch the sex center. And the posture is so erect that there is no gravitational pull. In this posture, one can forget the body completely because life energy is not flowing outward. The eyes are also to be closed or half-closed and the eyeballs still, because eyes are also a great outlet for energy.

Even in dreams you throw out much energy through eye movements. In fact, one way to know whether a person is dreaming or not is to put your fingers on his eyes. If they are moving, then he is dreaming. Awaken him, and you will find he was dreaming. If the eyeballs are not moving, then he is in deep, dreamless sleep, *sushupti.* All energy is going inward and nothing is going outward.

Asanas, pranayama—there are so many methods through which energies can be made to flow inward. When they flow inward they become one, because at the center there cannot be more than one. So the more energy goes inward, the more harmony there is. Conflicts drop. In the center there is no conflict. There is an organic unity of the whole. That is why bliss is felt.

Another thing: *asanas* and *pranayama* are bodily helps. They are important, but they are only physical helps. If your mind is in conflict then they will not be of much help, because body and mind are not two things really. They are two parts of one thing. You are not body and mind; you are body/mind. You are psycho/somatic or somato/psychic. We talk about the body as one thing and the mind as something different, but body and mind are two poles of one energy. The body is gross and the mind is subtle, but the energy is the same.

One has to work from both polarities. For the body there is *hatha* yoga: *asanas, pranayama,* etcetera; and for the mind there is *raja* yoga and other yogas that are basically concerned with your mental attitudes.

Body and mind are one energy. For example, if you can control your breath when you are angry, the anger will die. If you can go on breathing rhythmically, anger cannot overpower you. In the same way, if you go on breathing rhythmically, sexual passion cannot overpower you. It will be there, but it will not become manifest. No one will know it is there. Not even you will be able to know it. So sex can be suppressed; anger can be suppressed. Through rhythmic breathing you can suppress them so much that you yourself will not even be aware of it. But the anger or sex will still be there. The body has suppressed it, but it remains inside, untouched.

One has to work with both the body and the mind. The body should be trained through yogic methodology, and the mind through awareness. You will require more awareness if you practice yoga because things will become more subtle. If you are angry, you can ordinarily become aware of it because it is so gross. But if you practice *pranayama*, you will need more awareness, more acute sensitivity to be aware of anger, because now the anger will become more subtle. The body is not cooperating with it so there will be no physical expression of it at all.

If people practice awareness techniques and simultaneously practice yogic methods, they will know deeper realms of awareness. Otherwise they will be aware only of the gross. If you change the gross but do not change the subtle, you will be in a dilemma. Now conflict will assert itself in a new way.

Yoga is helpful, but it is only one part. The other part is what Buddha calls "mindfulness." Practice yoga so that the body becomes rhythmic and cooperative with your inner movements, and simultaneously practice mindfulness.

Be mindful of breathing. In yoga, you have to change the breathing process. In mindfulness, you have to be aware of the breathing as it is. Just be aware of it. If you can become aware of your breathing, then you can become aware of your thought process; otherwise not.

Those who try to become aware of their thought process directly, will not be able to do it. It will be very arduous, tedious. Breathing is the door to the mind. If you stop your breathing for a single moment, your thoughts will also stop. When breathing stops, the thought process stops. If your thinking is chaotic, your breathing will be chaotic. Breathing will simultaneously reflect your thought process.

Buddha talks about *anapanasati*: the yoga of awareness of the incoming and outgoing breath. He says, "Begin from here." And that is the correct beginning. One should begin from breathing and never from the thought process itself. When you can feel the subtle movements of breath, only then will you be able to feel the subtle movements of thought.

Awareness of the thought process will change the quality of the mind; *asanas* and *pranayama* will change the quality of the body. Then the moment comes when your body and mind are one, without any conflict at all. When they are synchronized, you are neither body nor mind. For the first time, you know yourself as the Self. You transcend.

You can transcend only when there is no conflict. In this harmonious moment when body and mind are one, with no conflict, you transcend both. You are neither. Now you are nothing in a sense: no-thing. You are simple consciousness. Not conscious of something, but just awareness itself.

This awareness without being aware of anything, this consciousness without being conscious of anything, is the moment of explosion. Your potential becomes actual. You explode into a new realm: the ultimate. This ultimate is the concern of all religions.

There are so many ways to reach this ultimate. One may talk about kundalini or not; it is immaterial. Kundalini is only a word. You can use another word. But what is signified by the word *kundalini* is bound to be there in some way or other as an inward flow of energy.

This inward flow is the only revolution, the only freedom. Otherwise you will go on creating more hells, because the more you go outward the further off you are from yourself. And the further off you are from yourself, the more ill and diseased you are.

Kundalini is the original source of all life, but you are cut off from it in so many ways. Then you become an outsider to yourself and you do not know how to come back home. This coming back is the science of yoga. As far as human transformation is concerned, kundalini yoga is the subtlest science.

You have asked why traditional methods are systematic and my method is chaotic. Traditional methods are systematic because the people in earlier times for whom they were developed were different. Modern man is a very new phenomenon. No traditional method can be used exactly as it exists, because modern man never existed before. So in a way, all traditional methods have become irrelevant.

For example, the body has changed so much. It is not as natural now as it was in the days when Patanjali developed his system of yoga. It is absolutely different. It is so drugged that no traditional method can be helpful.

In the past, medicine was not allowed to *hatha* yogis, absolutely not allowed, because chemical changes will not only make the methods difficult, but harmful. But the whole atmosphere is artificial now: the air, the water, the society, the living conditions. Nothing is natural. You are born in artificiality; you develop in it. So traditional methods will prove harmful today. They will have to be changed according to the modern situation.

Another thing: the quality of the mind has basically changed. In Patanjali's days, the center of the human personality was not the brain; it was the heart. And before that, it was not even the heart. It was still lower, near the navel. *Hatha* yoga developed methods which were useful, meaningful, to the person whose center of personality was the navel. Then, the center became the heart. Only then could *bhakti* yoga be used. *Bhakti* yoga developed in the middle ages because that is when the center of personality changed from the navel to the heart.

A method has to change according to the person to whom it is applied. Now, not even *bhakti* yoga is relevant. The center has gone even further from the navel. Now, the center is the brain. That is why teachings like those of Krishnamurti have appeal. No method is needed, no technique is needed—only understanding. But if it is just a verbal understanding, just intellectual, nothing changes, nothing is transformed. It again becomes an accumulation of knowledge.

I use chaotic methods rather than systematic ones because a chaotic method is very helpful in pushing the center down from the brain. The center cannot be pushed down through any systematic method because systemization is brain work. Through a systematic method, the brain will be strengthened; more energy will be added to it.

Through chaotic methods, the brain is nullified. It has nothing to do. The method is so chaotic that the center is automatically pushed from the brain to the heart. If you do my method of Dynamic Meditation vigorously, unsystematically, chaotically, your center moves to the heart.[1] Then there is a catharsis. A catharsis is needed because your heart is so suppressed, due to your brain. Your brain has taken over so much of your being that it dominates you. There is no place for the heart, so the longings of the heart are suppressed. You have never laughed heartily, never lived heartily, never done anything heartily. The brain always comes in to systematize, to make things mathematical, and the heart is suppressed.

So firstly, a chaotic method is needed to push the center of consciousness from the brain toward the heart. Then catharsis is needed to unburden the heart, to throw off suppressions, to make the heart open. If the heart becomes light and unburdened, then the center of consciousness is pushed still lower; it comes to the navel. The navel is the source of vitality, the seed source from which everything else comes: the body and the mind and everything.

I use this chaotic method very considerately. Systematic methodology will not help now, because the brain will use it as its own instrument. Nor can just the chanting of *bhajans* help now, because the heart is so burdened that it cannot flower into real chanting. Chanting can only be an escape for it; prayer can only be an escape. The heart cannot flower into prayer because it is so overburdened with suppressions. I have not seen a single person who can go deep into authentic prayer. Prayer is impossible because love itself has become impossible.

Consciousness must be pushed down to the source, to the roots. Only then is there the possibility of transformation. So I use chaotic methods to push the consciousness downward from the brain.

Whenever you are in chaos, the brain stops working. For example, if you are driving a car and suddenly someone runs in

[1] Dynamic Meditation and other techniques devised by Bhagwan are discussed in detail in *Meditation: The Art of Ecstasy*; Bhagwan Shree Rajneesh (New York: Harper & Row, Publishers, 1976.) Dynamic meditation consists of five ten-minute stages. The first is deep, fast, chaotic breathing to awaken the energy within. The second stage is a catharsis, a release of suppressions that have been made conscious by the breathing process. This is followed by a third stage: the vigorous repetition of the sound *hoo*, a sound that strikes the sex center and moves the energy upward. Then, ten or fifteen minutes of silence and stillness (the meditation); and ten or fifteen minutes of celebration, expressing the bliss that has been felt in the fourth stage, and, in gratitude, returning it to the universe.

front of you, you react so suddenly that it cannot be the work of the brain. The brain takes time. It thinks about what to do and what not to do. So whenever there is a possibility of an accident and you push the brake, you feel a sensation near your navel, as if it were your stomach that is reacting. Your consciousness is pushed down to the navel because of the accident. If the accident could be calculated beforehand, the brain would be able to deal with it; but when you are in an accident, something unknown happens. Then you notice that your consciousness has moved to the navel.

If you ask a Zen monk, "From where do you think?" he puts his hands on his stomach. When Westerners came into contact with Japanese monks for the first time, they could not understand. "What nonsense! How can you think from your stomach?" But the Zen reply is meaningful.* Consciousness can use any center of the body, and the center that is nearest to the original source is the navel. The brain is furthest away from the original source, so if life energy is moving outward, the center of consciousness will become the brain. And if life energy is moving inward, ultimately the navel will become the center.

Chaotic methods are needed to push the consciousness to its roots, because only from the roots is transformation possible. Otherwise you will go on verbalizing and there will be no transformation. It is not enough just to know what is right. You have to transform the roots; otherwise you will not change.

When a person knows the right thing and cannot do anything about it, he becomes doubly tense. He understands, but he cannot do anything. Understanding is meaningful only when it comes from the navel, from the roots. If you understand from the brain, it is not transforming.

The ultimate cannot be known through the brain, because when you are functioning through the brain you are in conflict with the roots from which you have come. Your whole problem is that you have moved away from the navel. You have come from the navel and you will die through it. One has to come back to the roots. But coming back is difficult, arduous.

* When we talk about a gut reaction, we mean an instinctive reaction that comes from the center of one's being—not from the mind but from the being itself. Presumably, the closer one lives to the center of his being, the more all of his reactions will come from that center and not from the mind. Ed.

Kundalini yoga is concerned with life energy and its inward flow. It is concerned with techniques to bring the body and mind to a point where transcendence is possible. Then, everything is changed. The body is different; the mind is different; the living is different. It is just *life*.

A bullock cart is useful, but it is no longer needed. Now you are driving a car, so you cannot use the technique that was used with the bullock cart. It was useful with the bullock cart, but it is irrelevant with the car.

Traditional methods have an appeal because they are so ancient and so many persons have achieved through them in the past. They may have become irrelevant to us, but they were not irrelevant to Buddha, Mahavir, Patanjali or Krishna. They were meaningful, helpful. The old methods may be meaningless now, but because Buddha achieved through them they have an appeal. The traditionalist feels: "If Buddha achieved through these methods, why can't I?" But we are in an altogether different situation now. The whole atmosphere, the whole thought-sphere, has changed. Every method is organic to a particular situation, to a particular mind, to a particular man.

The opposite extreme is that of Krishnamurti. He denies all methods. But to do that, he has to deny Buddha. It is the other aspect of the same coin. If you deny the methods then you have to deny Buddha, and if you do not deny Buddha then you cannot deny his methods.

These are extremes. Extremes are always wrong. You cannot deny a falsehood through taking an extreme position to it, because the opposite extreme will still be a falsehood. The truth always lies exactly in the middle. So to me, the fact that the old methods don't work doesn't mean that no method is useful. It only means that the methods themselves must change.

Even no-method is a method. It is possible that to someone only no-method will be a method. A method is always true in relation to a particular person; it is never general. When truths are generalized, they become false. So whenever anything is to be used or anything is to be said, it is always addressed to a particular human being: to his attention, to his mind, to him and no one else.

This too has become a difficulty now. In the old days there was always a one-to-one relationship between a teacher and a disciple. It was a personal relationship and a personal communication.

Today it is always impersonal. One has to talk to a crowd, so one has to generalize. But generalized truths become false. Something is meaningful only to a particular person.

I face this difficulty daily. If you come to me and ask me something, I answer *you* and no one else. Another time someone else asks me something, and I answer him and no one else. These two answers may even be contradictory, because the two persons who have asked may be contradictory. So if I am to help you, I must speak particularly to you. And if I speak particularly to each individual, I will have to say many conflicting things.

Any person who has been talking in general can be consistent, but then the truth becomes false, because every statement that is true is bound to be addressed to a particular person. Of course, the truth is eternal—it is never new, never old—but truth is the realization, the end. The means are always relevant or irrelevant to a particular person, to a particular mind, to a particular attitude.

As I see the situation, modern man has changed so much that he needs new methods, new techniques. Chaotic methods will help the modern mind because the modern mind is, itself, chaotic. This chaos, this rebelliousness in modern man is, in fact, a rebellion of other things: of the body against the mind and against its suppressions. If we talk about it in yogic terms we can say that it is the rebellion of the heart center and the navel center against the brain.

These centers are against the brain because the brain has monopolized the whole territory of the human soul. This cannot be tolerated any further. That is why universities have become centers of rebellion. It is not accidental. If the whole society is thought of as an organic body, then the university is the head, the brain.

Because of the rebelliousness of the modern mind, it is bound to be lenient toward loose and chaotic methods. Dynamic Meditation will help to move the center of consciousness away from the brain. Then the person using it will never be rebellious, because the cause of rebellion becomes fulfilled. He will be at ease.

So to me, meditation is not only a salvation for the individual, a transformation for the individual; it can also provide the groundwork for the transformation of the whole society, of the human being as such. Man will either have to commit suicide, or he will have to transform his energy.

5

Esoteric Games: A Hindrance to Growth

Is there a division between body and mind, matter and consciousness, the physical and the spiritual? How can one transcend body and mind to attain spiritual consciousness?

The first thing to be understood is that the division between body and mind is absolutely false. If you begin with that division you will reach nowhere; a false beginning leads nowhere. Nothing can come out of it because every step has its own logic of evolving. The second step will come out of the first, and the third out of the second and so on. There is a logical sequence. So the moment you take the first step, you have chosen everything in a way.

The first step is more important than the last, the beginning is more important than the end, because the end is just an outcome, a growth. But we are always concerned about the end, never with the beginning; always concerned with ends, never with means. The end has become so significant for us that we lose track of the seed, of the beginning. Then we can go on dreaming, but we will never reach the real.

To any seeker, this concept of a divided person, this concept of a dual existence—of body and mind, of the physical and the spiritual—is a false step. Existence is undivided; all divisions are just mental. The very way the mind looks at things creates a duality. It is the prison of the mind that divides.

Mind cannot do otherwise. It is difficult for the mind to conceive of two contradictions as one, of opposite polarities as one. The mind has a compulsion, an obsession to be consistent. It cannot conceive how light and darkness are one. It is inconsistent, paradoxical.

The mind has to create opposites: God and the devil, life and death, love and hate. How can you conceive of love and hate as one energy? It is difficult for the mind. So the mind divides. Then the difficulty is over. Hate is opposite to love, and love is opposite to hate. Now you can be consistent and the mind can be at ease. So division is a convenience of the mind—not a truth, not a reality.

It is convenient to divide yourself into two: the body and you. But the moment you divide, you have taken the wrong step. Unless you come back and change the first step, you can wander for lives and lives, and nothing will come of it; because one false step leads to more false steps. So begin with the right beginning. Remember that you and the body are not two, that two is just a convenience. One is enough as far as the existence is concerned.

It is artificial to divide yourself into two. Really, you always feel that you are one, but once you begin to think about it, the problem arises. If your body is hurt, in that very moment you never feel that you are two. You feel that you are one with the body. Only later, when you begin to think about it, do you divide.

In the present moment, there is no division. For example, if someone puts a dagger to your chest, at that moment there is no division. You do not think that he is going to kill your body; you think he is going to kill you. Only later, when it has become part of the memory, can you divide. Now you can look at things, think about them. You can say that the man was going to kill your body. But you cannot say it in the moment itself.

Whenever you feel, you feel oneness. Whenever you think, you begin to divide. Then, enmity is created. If you are not the body, a certain struggle develops. The question arises: "Who is the master? The body or me?" Then the ego begins to feel hurt. You begin to suppress the body. And when you suppress the body, you are suppressing yourself; when you fight with the body, you are fighting with yourself. So much confusion is created. It becomes suicidal.

Even if you try, you cannot really suppress your body. How can I suppress my left hand with my right hand? They look like two, but the same energy flows in both. If they were really two, then suppression would be possible—and not only suppression; absolute destruction would be possible—but if the same energy is flowing in both, how can I suppress my left hand? This is just make-believe. I can let my right hand put my left hand down, and I can pretend that my right hand has won, but the next second I can raise my left hand up and there will be nothing to stop it. This is the game we play. It goes on and on. Sometimes you push sex down, and sometimes sex pushes you down. It becomes a vicious circle. You can never suppress sex. You can transform it, but you can never suppress it.

Beginning with a division between you and the body leads to suppression. So if you are for transformation, you should not begin by dividing. Transformation can come only from an understanding of the whole *as the whole*. Suppression comes from misunderstanding the whole to be the divided parts. If I know that both hands are mine, then the effort to suppress one is absurd. The struggle becomes absurd, because which is to suppress which? Who is to fight whom? If you can feel at ease with your body, you can take a first step that will be the right one. Then division, suppression, will not come.

If you divide yourself from your body, many things will follow automatically. The more you suppress the body, the more frustrated you will be, because suppression is impossible. A momentary truce can be reached, but then you will be defeated again. And the more frustrated you become, the greater the division, the wider the gap that develops between you and the body. You begin to feel more and more inimical to it. You begin to feel that the body is very strong and that is why you are not capable of suppressing it. Then you think, "Now I will have to fight more vigorously!"

That is why I say that everything has its own logic. If you begin with an erroneous premise, you can go on and on to the very end, never reaching anywhere. Every struggle leads you to another struggle. The mind feels, "The body is strong and I am weak. I have to suppress it more." Or it feels, "I have to make my body weak now." All austerities are just efforts to make the body weak. But the more weak you make the body, the more weak you yourself become. The same relative strength is always maintained between you and your body.

The moment you become weak you begin to feel more frustrated, because now you are more easily defeated. And you cannot do anything about it: the weaker you get, the less possibility of overcoming the pull of the body and the more you have to fight it.

So the first thing is not to think in terms of division. This division—physical and spiritual, material and mental, consciousness and matter—is just a linguistic fallacy. The whole nonsense is created out of language.

For example, if you say something, I have to say "yes" or "no." We have no neutral attitude. "Yes" is always absolute; "no" is also absolute. There is no neutral word in any language. So De Bono has coined a new word: "po." He says "po" should come to be used as a neutral word. It means: "I have heard your point of view. I say neither 'yes' nor 'no' to it."

Use "po," and the whole possibility changes. "Po" is an artificial word that De Bono took from hy*po*thesis or *po*ssibility or *po*etry. It is a neutral word with no evaluation in it, with no condemnation, no appreciation, no commitment, neither for nor against. If someone is insulting you, just say "po." Then feel the difference inside you. A single word can make so much difference. When you say "po," you are saying, "I have heard you. Now I know that this is your attitude toward me. You may be right; you may be wrong. I am not making an evaluation."

Language creates division. Even great thinkers go on creating things linguistically that are not there. If you ask them, "What is mind?" they say, "It is not matter." If you ask them, "What is matter?" they say, "It is not mind." Neither matter nor mind is known. They define matter by mind and define mind by matter. The roots remain unknown. This is absurd, but it is more comforting to us than to say, "I don't know. Nothing is known about it."

When we say, "Mind is not matter," we feel at ease—as if something has been defined. Nothing has been defined. Mind and matter are both unknown, but to say, "I do not know," would be ego-deflating. The moment we divide, we feel we have become masters of things about which we are absolutely ignorant.

Ninety-nine percent of philosophy is created by language. Different languages create different sorts of philosophies, so if you change the language, the philosophy will change. That is why philosophy is not translatable. Science is always translatable, but philosophy is not. And poetry is even more untranslatable because it depends on a particular freshness of language. The moment you change the language, the flavor is lost; the taste is lost. That taste belongs to a particular arrangement of words, a particular use of words. They cannot be translated.

So the first thing to remember is not to begin with division. Only then do you begin rightly. I do not mean to begin with the concept that "I am one." I do not mean that. Then again you begin with a concept. Just begin in ignorance, in humble ignorance; with a basis of "I do not know."

You can say that body and mind are separate, or you can take the opposite position and can say, "I am one. Body and mind are one." But this statement still presupposes a division. You say "one," but you are feeling two. Against the feeling of two you assert oneness. This assertion is again a subtle suppression.

So do not begin with *advait*, with a nondual philosophy. Begin with existence, not with concepts. Begin with a deep, nonconceptualized consciousness. That is what I mean by a right beginning. Begin to feel the existential. Do not say "one" or "two"; do not say "this" or "that." Begin to feel what is. And you can only feel what is when the mind is not there, when concepts are not there, when philosophies and doctrines are not there—really, when language is not there. When language is absent, you are in the existence. When language is present, you are in the mind.

With a different language, you will have a different mind. There are so many languages. Not only linguistically but religiously, politically. A communist who is sitting by my side is not with me at all. He lives in a different language.

Just on the other side of me, someone may be sitting who believes in *karma*. The communist and this other man cannot meet. No dialogue is possible because they do not know each other's language at all. They may be using the same words, but still they do not know what the other is saying. They live in different universes.

With language, everyone lives in a private universe. Without language, you belong to the common tongue, the existence. This is what I mean by meditation: to drop out of the private linguisitic world and enter the nonverbal existence.

Those who divide body and mind are always against sex. The reason is that, ordinarily, sex is the only nonverbal, natural experience that we know. Language is not needed at all. If you use language in sex, you cannot go deep in it. So all those who say you are not the body will be against sex, because in sex you are absolutely undivided.

Do not live in a verbal world. Move deeply into existence itself. Use anything, but come back again and again to the level of the nonverbal, the level of consciousness. With trees, with birds, with the sky, the sun, the clouds, the rain—live with the nonverbal existence everywhere. And the more you do it, the more deeply you go into it, the more you will feel a oneness that does not exist in opposition to twoness; a oneness that is not just a joining of two but is the oneness of the mainland with an island that joins the mainland below the surface of the ocean water. The two have always been one. You see them as two because you look only at the surface.

Language is the surface. All types of language (religious, political) are on the surface. When you live with the nonverbal existence, you come to a subtle oneness that is not a mathematical oneness but an existential oneness.

So do not try to play these verbal games: "Body and mind are divided"; "Body and mind are one." Drop them! They are interesting, but useless. They lead nowhere. Even if you find some truth in them, they are only verbal truths. What are you going to learn from them? For thousands of years your mind has played this game, but it is childish; any verbal game is childish. However seriously you play it makes no difference. You can find many things to support your position, many meanings, but it is just a game. As far as day-to-day work is concerned, language is useful; but you cannot move into the deeper realms with it, because these realms are nonverbal.

Language is just a game. If you find some associations between the verbal and the nonverbal, the reason is not that you have found some important secret, no. You can find many associations that look important, but they are not really significant. They are there because your mind has unconsciously created them.

The human mind everywhere is basically similar, so everything that develops out of the human mind tends to be similar. For example, the word for "mother" happens to be similar in every language. Not because there is anything significant about it, but because the sound *ma* is the sound that is most easily uttered by every child. Once the sound is there you can create different words out of it, but a sound is just a sound. The child is just making the sound *ma*, but you hear it as a word.

Sometimes a similarity can be found that is just coincidental. "God" is the reverse of "dog." It's just a coincidence. But we find it meaningful because to us a dog is something mean. Then we say that God is the reverse of this. This is our interpretation. It may be that for the opposite of God we created a word ("dog") and then gave this name to dogs. The two are not related at all, but if you can create a relationship between them, it appears significant to you.

You can go on creating similarities out of anything. You can create a vast ocean of words, with infinite similarities. For instance, the word "monkey." You can play with this word and find certain associations, but before Darwin this would have been impossible. Because we now know that man comes from the monkey, we can play word games. We can say "monkey" ("man-key"): the key to man. Other people have joined these two words in a different way. They have said, "Monkey and man are related because of the mind. Man has a monkeyish mind."

So you can create associations and enjoy it, you can feel it is a good game, but it is just a game. One must remember that. Otherwise you will lose track of what is real and what is just a game, and you will go mad.

The more deeply you go into words, the more associations you will find. And then, just by tricks and turns, you can create a whole philosophy out of it. Many do that. Even Ram Dass has done this very much. He has played with the word "monkey" in this way; he has compared "dog" and "God" in this way. It is all right; there is nothing wrong in it. What I am saying is this: if you are playing a game and enjoying it, then enjoy it—but never be fooled by it. And you *can* be fooled. The game can be so engrossing that you will go on with it, and much energy will be wasted.

People think that because there are so many similarities among languages there must have been an original language out of which all other languages have come. But these similarities are not there because of a common language; they are there because of similarities in the human mind. All over the world, people who are frustrated make the same sounds; people who are in love make the same sounds. A basic similarity among human beings creates a certain similarity in our words also. But don't take it seriously, because then you can lose yourself in it. Even if you find some significant sources it is meaningless, irrelevant. For a spiritual seeker, it is beside the point.

And our minds are such that when we go to seek something we begin with a preconception. If I feel that Muslims are bad, then I go on finding things that support my argument and ultimately I prove myself right. Then whenever I meet a Muslim I begin to find faults, and no one can say I am wrong because I have "proof."

Someone can come to the same individual with a contradictory concept. If Muslim means "a good man" to him, proof of this goodness can be found with this same Muslim. Good and bad are not opposites; they exist together. Man has the possibility to be either, so whatever you are looking for in him you will be able to find. In some situations he will be good and in some situations he will be bad. When you judge him, it depends more on your definition than on the situation itself. It depends on how you look at this or that.

If you think smoking is bad, for example, then it becomes bad. If you think that to behave in a particular way is bad, then it becomes bad. If we are sitting here and someone falls asleep while we are talking, if you think it is bad it is bad. But really, nothing is good; nothing is bad. Someone with a different attitude will think that this same thing is good. He will think that if someone lies down and goes to sleep among friends, it is good that he feels the freedom to do it. So it depends on your attitude.

I was reading about some of the experiments that A. S. Neill tried at his school, Summerhill. He experimented with a new type of school where there was total freedom. He was the headmaster, but there was no discipline. One day a teacher was sick so he told the boys not to create any nuisance to disturb the teacher that night.

But at night, the boys began fighting right next to the sick man's room. Neill went upstairs. When the children heard someone was coming they became silent and began studying. Neill looked into the room through the window. One boy, who had been pretending to get ready for bed, looked up and saw him at the window. He said to the others, "It's no one but Neill. Come on, there's no need to stop. It's only Neill." So they began to fight again. And Neill was the headmaster!

Neill wrote, "I was so happy that they were so unafraid of me that they were able to say, 'There is no need to worry. It's only Neill.'" He felt good about it, but no other headmaster would have felt good. No other headmaster! Never in history!

So it depends on you, on how you define things. Neill felt it as love but, again, that is his definition. We always find what we are looking for. You can find anything in the world if you are seriously in search of it.

So do not begin with a mind fixed on finding something. Just begin! An inquiring mind does not mean to be in search of anything but simply to be searching. Simply searching, with no preconceived notions, with nothing definite to find. We find things because we are looking for them.

The meaning of the Biblical story of the Tower of Babel is that the moment you speak, you are divided. The story is not that people began to speak different languages but that they began to speak at all. The moment you speak, confusion is there. The moment you utter something, you are divided. Only silence is one.

Many people have wasted their lives seeking things. When something is taken seriously, you can waste your life very easily. Playing with words is so ego-fulfilling that you can waste your life doing it. Even if it is interesting—a good game, amusing—it is useless for a spiritual seeker. The spiritual search is not a game.

The same game can be played with numbers. You can make connections. You can figure out why there are seven days in the week, seven musical notes, seven spheres, seven bodies. Why is there always seven? Then you can create a philosophy around it, but this philosophy will just be a product of your imagination.

Sometimes things begin in very innocent ways. For example, the way counting began. The only reason there are nine digits is because man has ten fingers. All over the world, the first counting that happened was on the fingers. So ten was the chosen limit. It was enough, because then you can go on repeating. So all over the world, there are nine digits.

Once nine has been fixed upon, it becomes difficult to conceive of how to proceed with more than nine digits or less. But less can be used. Nine is only a habit. Leibnitz used only three digits: 1, 2 and 3. Any problem can be solved with three digits as well as nine. Einstein used only two digits: 1 and 2. Then counting becomes: 1, 2, 10, 11. . . . For us, there seems to be a gap of eight, but that gap doesn't exist; it is just in our minds.

We have a fixed attitude that 3 must come after 2. There is no must. But it becomes confusing to us. We think that 2 and 2 is always 4, but there is no inherent necessity in it. If you use a two digit system, then 2 and 2 will be 11. But then "11" and "4" mean the same thing. You can say that two chairs and two chairs are four chairs, or you can say they are eleven chairs, but whatever system you decide to follow, existentially the number of chairs remains the same.

You can find reasons for everything—why there are seven days in a week, why there are twenty-eight days in a woman's menstrual cycle, why there are seven notes in the scale, why there are seven spheres. And some of these things may actually have a reason behind them.

For example, the word "menses" means a month. It is possible that man first began counting months according to the menstrual cycle of women, because the natural feminine cycle is a fixed time period: twenty-eight days. This would have been an easy method to know that one month had passed. When your wife begins her menses, one month has gone by.

Or, you can count the months according to the moon. But then the time period that we call "one month" changes to thirty days. The moon gets bigger for fifteen days and wanes for fifteen days, so in thirty days it has gone through its complete cycle.

We fix the months according to the moon, so we say that a month has thirty days. But if you determine it by Venus or by the menstrual period, it will have twenty-eight days. You can dissolve the disparity by dividing the twenty-eight day cycle and thinking in terms of a seven-day week. Then, once this division becomes fixed in the mind, other things follow automatically. That is what I mean: everything has its own logic. Once you have a seven-day week you can find many other patterns of seven, and seven becomes a significant number, a magical number. It is not. Either the whole life is magical or nothing is. It becomes just a game for the imagination.

You can play with these things, and there will be many coincidences. The world is so big, so infinite, so many things are happening every second, that there are bound to be coincidences. The coincidences begin to add up, and finally you have created so long a list that you are convinced by it. Then you wonder, "Why is there always seven? There must be some mystery to it." The mystery is only that your mind sees the coincidences and tries to interpret them in a logical way.

Gurdjieff said that man is food for the moon. This is perfectly logical. It shows the foolishness of logic. Everything in life is good for something else, so Gurdjieff came upon a very inventive idea: that man must also be food for something. Then, "What is man food for?" becomes a logical question to ask.

The sun cannot be the eater of man because the sun's rays are food for other things, for plants. Man would then be on a lower rung than other species. But this cannot be so because man is the highest animal—according to himself. So, man cannot be food for the sun.

The moon is related to us in a subtle way, but not in the way Gurdjieff said. It is subtly related to women's menstrual periods. It is related to the tide, to the ebb and flow of the sea. More people seem to go mad on the full moon. That is where the word "lunatic" comes from: lunar (the moon).

The moon has always hypnotized man's mind. Gurdjieff said, "Man must be food for the moon, because food can be easily hypnotized by the eater." Animals, snakes in particular, first hypnotize their victims. They become so paralyzed that they can be eaten. This is another coincidence that Gurdjieff played with. Poets, lunatics, aesthetes, thinkers, are all hypnotized by the moon. Something *must* be there. Man *must* be a food.

You can play with this idea. With a fertile mind like Gurdjieff's, things go on falling into a logical pattern. Gurdjieff was a genius who could put things in such a way that they appeared to be logical, rational, meaningful, no matter how absurd they were. He postulated this theory and then his imagination was able to find many connections, many proofs.

Every system-maker uses logic to distort, to prove his point. Every system-maker! Those who want to remain with the truth cannot create systems. For example, I could never create a system because, to me, the very effort is wrong. I can only be fragmentary in what I say, incomplete. There will be gaps, unbridgeable ones. With me, you will have to jump from one point to the next.

A system can be created very easily because the gaps can be filled in by the imagination. Then the whole thing becomes very clean and neat, logical. But as it becomes logical, it moves further and further away from the existential source.

The more you know, the more you feel that there are gaps that cannot be filled. Existence can never be consistent, never. A system needs to be consistent, but existence itself is never consistent. So no system can ever explain it.

Wherever man has created systems to explain existence (in India, in Greece, in China), he has created games. If you accept the first step as true, then the whole system works perfectly; but if you don't accept the first step, the whole edifice falls down. The whole edifice is an exercise in imagination. It is good. Poetic, beautiful. But once a system insists that its version of existence is the absolute truth, it becomes violent and destructive. These systems of truth are poetries. They are beautiful, but they are just poetry. Many gaps have been filled in by the imagination.

Gurdjieff was indicating certain fragments of the truth, but because it is not so easy to rest a theory on one or two fragments, he assembled many fragments. Then he tried to make these fragments into a coherent system. He began to fill in the gaps. But the more the gaps are filled in, the more the reality is lost. And ultimately, the whole system falls because of those filled-in gaps.

One who is enchanted with the personality of a teacher may not become aware of the gaps in his theory, while those who are not enchanted will see only the gaps and not the fragments of truth. For his followers, Buddha is a Buddha (an enlightened one), but for others he creates confusion because they see only the gaps. If you join all the gaps together it becomes destructive, but if you join all the fragments of truth together, it can become a foundation for your transformation.

Truth is bound to be fragmentary. It is so infinite that with a finite mind you can never get to the whole. And if you insist on trying to get to the whole, you will lose your mind, you will transcend your mind. But if you create a system, you will never lose your mind, because then your mind fills in the gaps. The system becomes neat and clean; it becomes impressive, rational, understandable, but never anything more. And something more is needed: the force, the energy to transform you. But that force can come only through fragmentary glimpses.

Mind creates so many systems, so many methods. It thinks, "If I drop out of the life I am leading, something deeper will be found." This is absurd. But the mind goes on thinking that somewhere in Tibet, somewhere in Meru Pravat, somewhere, the "real thing" must be happening. The heart is in conflict: how to go there? How to come in contact with the masters who are working there? The mind is always looking for something somewhere else, never for something here and now. The mind is never *here*. And each theory attracts people: "On Meru Mountain, the real thing is happening right now! Go there, be in contact with the masters there, and you will be transformed."

Don't be a victim to such things. Even if they have some basis, don't fall for them. Someone may be telling you something that is real, but the reason for your attraction is wrong. The real is here and now; it is with you now. Just work on yourself. Even when one has gone to every Meru Mountain, one has to come back to oneself. Ultimately, one finds that Meru Mountain is here, Tibet is here: "Here, inside me. And I have been wandering and wandering everywhere. . . ."

The more rational the system, the more it falls apart and something irrational must be introduced. But the moment you introduce the irrational element, the mind begins to shatter. So do not worry about systems. Just take a jump into the here and now.

6

The Psychology of Dreams

Can you explain what you mean by dreams?

We have seven bodies: 1) the physical, 2) the etheric, 3) the astral, 4) the mental, 5) the spiritual, 6) the cosmic, and 7) the nirvanic. Each body has its own type of dream. The physical body is known in Western psychology as the conscious, the etheric body as the unconscious and the astral body as the collective unconscious.

The physical body creates its own dreams. If your stomach is upset, a particular type of dream is created. If you are unhealthy, feverish, the physical body creates its own type of dream. One thing is certain: the dream is created out of some dis/ease.

Physical discomfort, physical dis/ease, creates its own realm of dreams, so a physical dream can even be stimulated from the outside. You are sleeping. If a wet cloth is put around your legs, you will begin to dream. You may dream you are crossing a river. If a pillow is put on your chest, you will begin to dream. You may dream that someone is sitting on you, or a stone has fallen on you. These are dreams that come through the physical body.

The etheric body (the second body) dreams in its own way.* These etheric dreams have created much confusion in Western psychology. Freud misunderstood etheric dreams for dreams caused by suppressed desires. There *are* dreams that are caused by suppressed desires, but these dreams belong to the first body, the physical. If you have suppressed physical desires—if you have fasted for instance—then there is every possibility that you will dream of breakfast. Or, if you have suppressed sex, then there is

* In the East, the etheric body is known as the vital body, the energy body. For most of us it is unconscious, but Bhagwan explains in the following three chapters how the etheric body (and the higher bodies) can be made conscious.

every possibility that you will have sexual fantasies. But these dreams belong to the first body. The etheric body is left out of psychological investigation, so its dreams are interpreted as belonging to the first body, the physical. Then, much confusion is created.

The etheric body can travel in dreams. There is every possibility of it leaving your body. When you remember it, it is remembered as a dream, but it is not a dream in the same sense as the dreams of the physical body. The etheric body can go out of you when you are asleep. Your physical body will be there, but your etheric body can go out and travel in space. There is no space limiting it; there is no question of distance for it. Those who do not understand this, who do not recognize the existence of the etheric body, may interpret this as the realm of the unconscious. They divide man's mind into conscious and unconscious. Then physiological dreaming is called "conscious" and etheric dreaming is called "unconscious." It is not unconscious. It is as conscious as physiological dreaming, but conscious on another level. If you become conscious of your etheric body, the dreaming concerned with that realm becomes conscious.

Just as physiological dreams can be created from the outside, so too can etheric dreams be created, stimulated. *Mantra* is one of the methods to create etheric visions, etheric dreams. A particular *mantra* or a particular *nada* (a particular word, sounding repeatedly in the etheric center) can create etheric dreams. There are so many methods. Sound is one of them.

Sufis have used perfume to create etheric visions. Mohammed himself was very fond of perfume. A particular perfume can create a particular dream.

Colors can also be of help. Leadbeater once had an etheric dream of blueness—just blueness, but of a particular shade.* He began to search for that particular blue all over the markets of the world. After several years of search, it was finally found in an Italian shop—a velvet of that particular shade. The velvet was then used to create etheric dreams in others as well.

So when someone goes deep in meditation and sees colors, and experiences perfumes and sounds and music absolutely unknown,

* Leadbeater, one of the leading figures of the early Theosophical movement, played an instrumental role in the spiritual training of Krishnamurti.

these too are dreams, dreams of the etheric body. So-called spiritual visions belong to the etheric body; they are etheric dreams. Gurus revealing themselves before their disciples is nothing but etheric travel, etheric dreaming. But because we have only searched the mind at one level of existence, the physiological, these dreams have either been interpreted in the language of the physiological or discarded, neglected.

Or, put into the unconscious. To say that anything is part of the unconscious is really just to admit that we do not know anything about it. It is a technicality, a trick. Nothing is unconscious, but everything that is conscious on a deeper level is unconscious on the previous level. So for the physical, the etheric is unconscious; for the etheric, the astral is unconscious; for the astral, the mental is unconscious. "Conscious" means that which is known; "unconscious" means that which is still not known, the unknown.

There are also astral dreams. In astral dreaming you go into your previous births. That is your third dimension of dreaming.

Sometimes in an ordinary dream, part of the etheric or part of the astral may be there. Then the dream becomes a muddle, a mess; you cannot understand it. Because your seven bodies are in existence simultaneously, something from one realm can pass into another, can penetrate it. So sometimes, even in ordinary dreams, there are fragments of the etheric or astral.

In the first body, the physical, you can travel in neither time nor space. You are confined to your physical state and to the particular time it is—say, ten o'clock at night. Your physical body can dream in this particular time and space, but not beyond it. In the etheric body you can travel in space but not in time. You can go anywhere, but the time is still ten o'clock at night. In the astral realm, in the third body, you can travel not only in space but also in time. The astral body can trespass the barrier of time—but only toward the past, not toward the future. The astral mind can go into the whole infinite series of the past, from amoeba to man.

In Jungian psychology, the astral mind has been called the collective unconscious. It is your individual history of births. Sometimes it penetrates into ordinary dreams, but more often in pathological states than in healthy ones. In a man who is mentally diseased, the first three bodies lose their usual distinction from one another. A person who is mentally ill may dream about his previous births, but no one will believe him. He himself will not believe it. He will say it is just a dream.

This is not dreaming on the physical plane. It is astral dreaming. And astral dreaming has much meaning, much significance. But the third body can dream only about the past, not about what is to be.

The fourth body is the mental. It can travel into the past and into the future. In an acute emergency, sometimes even an ordinary person can have a glimpse of the future. If someone near and dear to you is dying, the message may be delivered to you in an ordinary dream. Because you do not know any other dimension of dreaming, because you do not know the other possibilities, the message will penetrate your ordinary dreaming.

But the dream will not be clear because of barriers that have to be crossed before the message can become a part of your ordinary dreaming state. Each barrier eliminates something, transforms something. Each body has its own symbology so every time a dream passes from one body to another it is translated into the symbology of that body. Then, everything becomes confused.

If you dream in the fourth body in a *clear-cut* way—not through another body but through the fourth body itself—then you can penetrate into the future. But only into your own future. It is still individual; you cannot penetrate into another's person's future.

For the fourth body, the past is as much the present as the future is the present. Past, future and present become one. Everything becomes a *now*: *now* penetrating backward, *now* penetrating forward. There is no past and no future, but there is still time. Time, even as "the present," is still a flowing of time. You will still have to focus your mind. You can see toward the past, but you will have to focus your mind in that direction. Then the future and the present will be held in abeyance. When you focus toward the future, the other two—past and present—will be absent. You will be able to see past, present and future, but not as one. And you will be able to see only your own individual dreams, dreams that belong to *you* as an individual.

The fifth body, the spiritual body, crosses the realm of the individual and the realm of time. Now you are in eternity. The dreaming is not concerned with you as such, but with the consciousness of the whole. Now you know the entire past of the whole existence, but not the future.

Through this fifth body, all myths of creation have been developed. They are all the same. The symbols differ, the stories differ a little bit, but whether they are Christian or Hindu or Jewish or Egyptian, the myths of creation—how the world was created, how it came into existence—are all parallel; they all have an undercurrent of similarity. For example, similar stories of the great flood exist all over the world. There is no historical record of them but, still, there *is* a record. That record belongs to the fifth mind, the spiritual body. The fifth mind can dream about them.

The more you penetrate inward, the more the dream comes nearer and nearer to reality. Physiological dreaming is not so real. It has its own reality, but it is not so real. The etheric is much more real, the astral is even more real, the mental *approximates* the real and finally, in the fifth body, you become authentically realistic in your dreaming. This is the way to know reality. To call it dreaming is not adequate. But in a way it is dreaming, because the real is not objectively present. It has its own objectivity, but it comes as a subjective experience.

Two persons who have realized the fifth body can dream simultaneously, which is not possible before this. Ordinarily there is no way of dreaming a common dream, but from the fifth body onward, a dream can be dreamt by many persons simultaneously. That is why the dreams are objective in a way. We can compare notes. That is how so many persons, dreaming in the fifth body, came to know the same myths. These myths were not created by single individuals. They were created by particular schools, particular traditions working together.

So the fifth type of dreaming becomes much more real. The four preceding types are unreal in a sense because they are individual. There is no possibility of another person sharing the experience; there is no way to judge the validity of it—whether it is a fantasy or not. A fantasy is something you have projected; a dream is something that is not in existence as such, but which you have come to know. As you go inward, the dreaming becomes less fantastic, less imaginary—more objective, more real, more authentic.

All theological concepts are created by the fifth body. They differ in their language, their terminology, their conceptualization, but they are basically the same. They are dreams of the fifth body.

In the sixth body, the cosmic body, you cross the threshold of conscious/unconscious, matter/mind. You lose all distinctions. The sixth body dreams about the cosmos. You cross the threshold of consciousness and the unconscious world also becomes conscious. Now everything is alive and conscious. Even what we call matter is now part of consciousness.

In the sixth body, dreams of cosmic myths have been realized. You have transcended the individual, you have transcended the conscious, you have transcended time and space, but language is still possible. It points toward something; it indicates something. Theories of Brahma, *maya*, theories of oneness, of the infinite, have all been realized in the sixth type of dreaming. Those who have dreamt in the cosmic dimension have been the creators of the great systems, the great religions.

Through the sixth type of mind, dreams are in terms of being, not in terms of nonbeing; in terms of positive existence, not in terms of nonexistence. There is still a clinging to existence and a fear of nonexistence. Matter and mind have become one, but not existence and nonexistence, not being and nonbeing. They are still separate. This is the last barrier.

The seventh body, the nirvanic, crosses the boundary of the positive and jumps into nothingness. It has its own dreams: dreams of nonexistence, dreams of nothingness, dreams of the void. The *yes* has been left behind, and even the *no* is not a *no* now; the nothingness is not nothing. Rather, the nothing is even more infinite. The positive must have boundaries; it cannot be infinite. Only the negative has no boundaries.

So the seventh body has its own dreams. Now there are no symbols, no forms. Only the formless is. Now there is no sound but the soundless; there is absolute silence. These dreams of silence are total, unending.

These are the seven bodies. Each of them has its own dreams. But these seven dimensions of dreams can become a hindrance in knowing the seven types of realities.

Your physiological body has a way to know the real and a way to dream about it. When you take your food, this is a reality; but when you dream that you are taking food, it is not a reality. The dream is a substitute for the real food. So the physiological body has its own reality and its own way of dreaming. These are two different ways in which the physiological functions, and they are very far apart from one another.

The more you go toward the center—the higher the body you are in—the nearer dream and reality are to one another. Just like lines drawn from the periphery toward the center of a circle come nearer as they approach the center, and are further apart as they go toward the circumference, so too dream and reality come nearer and nearer as you go toward your center and they become further and further apart as you go toward the periphery. So as far as the physiological body is concerned, dreaming and reality are far apart. The distance between them is great. Dreams are just fantasy.

This separation will not be so great in the etheric body. The real and the dream will come nearer, so to know what is real and what is a dream will be more difficult than in the physiological body. But still, the difference can be known. If your etheric travel has been real travel it will happen while you are awake. If it has been a dream it will happen when you are asleep. To know the difference, you will have to be awakened in the etheric body.

There are methods to be aware in your etheric body. All methods of inner working such as *japa* (the repetition of a *mantra*) disconnect you from the outside world. If you fall asleep, the constant repetition can create a hypnotic sleep. Then, you will dream. But if you can remain aware of your *japa* and it does not create a hypnotic effect in you, then you will know the real as far as the etheric is concerned.

In the third body, the astral, it is even more difficult to know the difference because the two have come even closer. If you have known the real astral body and not just astral dreaming, then you will go beyond the fear of death. From here, one knows one's immortality. But if the astral is a dream and not real, then you will be crippled by the fear of death. This is the point of distinction, the touchstone: the fear of death.

A person who believes that the soul is immortal and goes on repeating and repeating it, convincing himself, will not be able to know the distinction between what is real in the astral body and what is an astral dream. One should not believe in immortality;

one should *know* it. But before knowing, one must have doubts about it, uncertainty about it. Only then will you know whether you really *know* it or whether you have just projected it. If it is your belief that the soul is immortal, the belief may penetrate your astral mind. Then you will begin to dream, but it will just be a dream. But if you have no belief, just a thirst to know, to seek—without knowing what is to be sought, without knowing what will be found, without any preconceptions or prejudices—if you are just seeking in a vacuum, then you will know the difference. So people who believe in the immortality of the soul, in past lives, those who accept them on faith, may just be dreaming on the astral plane and not knowing the real.

In the fourth body, the mental, dream and reality become neighbors. Their faces are so alike that there is every possibility that one will be judged to be the other. The mental body can have dreams that are as realistic as the real. And there are methods to create such dreams—yogic, tantric and other methods. A person who is practicing fasting, loneliness, darkness, will create the fourth type of dreams, mental dreams. They will be so real, more real than the reality that is surrounding us.

In the fourth body, the mind is totally creative—unhindered by anything objective, unhindered by material boundaries. Now it is totally free to create. Poets, painters, all live in the fourth type of dreaming; all art is produced by the fourth type of dreaming. A person who can dream in the fourth realm can become a great artist. But not one who knows.

In the fourth body, one must be aware of any type of mental creation. One should not project anything; otherwise it will be projected. One should not wish anything; otherwise there is every possibility that the wish will be the fulfillment. Not only inwardly. Even outwardly the wish can be fulfilled. In the fourth body, the mind is so powerful, so crystal clear, because the fourth body is the last home for the mind. Beyond this, no-mind begins.

The fourth body is the original source of the mind, so you can create anything. One must constantly be aware that there is no wish, no imagination, no image; no god, no guru. Otherwise they will all be created out of you. You will be the creator! It is so blissful to see them that one longs to create them. This is the last barrier for the *sadhaka*, the seeker. If one crosses this, he will not face a greater barrier.

If you are aware, if you are just a witness in the fourth body, then you know the real. Otherwise you go on dreaming. And no reality is comparable to these dreams. They will be ecstatic; no ecstasy is comparable. So one must be aware of ecstasy, of happiness, of blissfulness, and one must constantly be aware of any type of image. The moment there is an image, the fourth mind begins to flow into a dream. One image leads to the next, and you go on dreaming.

The fourth type of dreaming can only be prevented if you are a witness. Witnessing makes the difference, because if dreaming is there you will be identified with it. Identification is dreaming as far as the fourth body is concerned. In the fourth body, awareness and the witnessing mind are the path toward the real.

In the fifth body the dream and the real become one. Every type of duality is cast off. There is no question of any awareness now. Even if you are unaware, you will be aware of your unawareness. Now dreaming becomes just a reflection of the real. There is a difference, but no distinction. If I see myself in the mirror, there is no distinction between me and the reflection, but there is a difference. I am the real and the reflected one is not real.

The fifth mind, if it has cultivated different concepts, may have the illusion of knowing itself because it has seen itself reflected in the mirror. It *will* be knowing itself, but not as it is—only as it is reflected. This is the only difference. But in a way, it is dangerous. The danger is that you may become satisfied with the reflection, and the mirrorlike image will be taken as the real.

As far as the fifth body itself is concerned, there is no real danger if this happens, but it is a danger as far as the sixth body is concerned. If you have seen yourself only in the mirror, then you cannot cross the boundary of the fifth and go to the sixth. You cannot pass any boundary through a mirror. So there have been persons who have remained in the fifth. Those who say that there are infinite souls and each soul has its own individuality—these persons have remained in the fifth. They have known themselves, but not immediately, not directly—only through the medium of a mirror.

Where does this mirror come from? It comes through the cultivation of concepts: "I am the soul. Eternal, immortal. Beyond death, beyond birth." To conceive of oneself as the soul without *knowing* it is to create a mirror. Then you will not know yourself as you are, but as you are mirrored through your concepts. The only difference will be this: if the knowledge is coming through a mirror it is a dream and if it is direct, immediate, without any mirror, then it is real. This is the only difference, but it is a great one—not in relation to the bodies that you have crossed, but in relation to the bodies that are still to be penetrated.

How can one be aware whether he is dreaming in the fifth or living the real? There is only one way: to drop every type of scripture, to take leave of every type of philosophy. Now there should be no more guru; otherwise the guru will become a mirror. From here on, you are totally alone. No one can be taken as a guide or the guide will become a mirror.

From now on, the aloneness is total and complete. Not loneliness but aloneness. Loneliness is always concerned with others; aloneness is concerned with oneself. I feel lonely when there is no link between me and anyone else, but I feel alone when I *am*.

Now one should be alone in every dimension: words, concepts, theories, philosophies, doctrines; gurus, scriptures; Christianity, Hinduism; Buddha, Christ, Krishna, Mahavir. One should be alone now; otherwise anything that is present will become a mirror. Buddha will become a mirror now. Very dear, but very dangerous.

If you are absolutely alone, there will be nothing in which you can be reflected. So meditation is the word for the fifth body. It means to be totally alone, free from every type of mentation. It means to be with no mind. If there is any type of mind it will become a mirror and you will be reflected in it. One should now be a no-mind, with no thinking, no contemplation.

In the sixth body there is no mirror. Now only the cosmic is. You have been lost. You are no more; the dreamer is not. But the dream can still exist without the dreamer. And when there is a dream without the dreamer, it looks like authentic reality. There is no mind, no one to think, so whatever is known is *known*. It becomes your knowledge. Myths of creation come; they float by. You are not; things are just floating by. No one is there to judge; no one is there to dream.

But a mind that is not, still *is*. A mind that is annihilated still exists—not as an individual, but as the cosmic whole. You are not, but the Brahma is. That is why they say that the whole world is a dream of the Brahma. This whole world is a dream, *maya*. Not a dream of any individual, but a dream of the total, the whole. You are not, but the total is dreaming.

Now the only distinction is whether the dream is positive. If it is positive it is illusory, it is a dream, because in an ultimate sense only the negative is. When everything has become part of the formless, when everything has come back to the original source, then everything *is* and at the same time *is not*. The positive is the only factor remaining. It must be jumped over.

So if, in the sixth body, the positive is lost, you penetrate into the seventh. The real of the sixth is the door of the seventh. If there is nothing positive—no myth, no image—then the dream has ceased. Then there is only *what is*: suchness. Now nothing exists but existence. Things are not, but the source is. The tree is not, but the seed is.

Those who have known have called this type of mind *samadhi* with seed (*samadhi sabeej*). Everything has been lost; everything has returned to the original source, the cosmic seed. The tree is not, but the seed is. But from the seed, dreaming is still possible, so even the seed must be destroyed.

In the seventh, there is neither dream nor reality. You can only see something real up to the point where dreaming is possible. If there is no possibility of dreams, then neither the real nor the illusory exists. So the seventh is the center. Now, dream and reality have become one. There is no difference. Either you dream of nothingness or you know nothingness, but the nothingness remains the same.

If I dream about you it is illusory. If I see you it is real. But if I dream about your absence or I *see* your absence, there is no difference. If you dream about the absence of anything, the dream will be the same as the absence itself. Only in terms of something positive is there a real difference. So up to the sixth body there is a difference. In the seventh body only nothingness remains. There is an absence even of the seed. This is *nirbeej samadhi*, seedless *samadhi*. Now there is no possibility of dreaming.

So there are seven types of dreams and seven types of realities. They penetrate one another. Because of this, there is much confusion. But if you make a distinction between the seven, if you become clear about it, it will help much. Psychology is still far away from knowing about dreams. What it knows is only about the physiological, and sometimes the etheric. But the etheric too is interpreted as the physiological.

Jung has penetrated a little deeper than Freud, but his analysis of the human mind is treated as mythological, religious. Still, he has the seed. If Western psychology is to develop, it is through Jung not Freud. Freud was the pioneer, but every pioneer becomes a barrier for further progress if attachment to his advances becomes an obsession. Even though Freud is out of date now, Western psychology is still obsessed with its Freudian beginning. Freud must become part of history now. Psychology must proceed further.

In America, they are trying to learn about dreaming through laboratory methods. There are many dream laboratories, but the methods used are concerned only with the physiological. Yoga, tantra and other esoteric training must be introduced if the whole world of dreams is to be known. Every type of dream has a parallel type of reality and if the whole *maya* cannot be known, if the whole world of illusions cannot be known, then it is impossible to know the real. It is only through the illusory that the real can be known.

But do not take what I have said as a theory, a system. Just make it a starting point, and begin to dream with a conscious mind. Only when you become conscious in your dreams can the real be known.

We are not conscious even of our physical body. We remain unaware of it. Only when some part is diseased do we become aware. One must become aware of the body in health. To be aware of the body in disease is just an emergency measure. It is a natural, built-in process. Your mind must be aware when some part of the body is diseased so that it can be taken care of, but the moment it becomes all right again you become sleepy about it.

You must become aware of your own body: its workings, its subtle feelings, its music, its silences. Sometimes the body is silent; sometimes it is noisy; sometimes relaxed. The feeling is so different in each state that it is unfortunate we are not aware of it. When you are going to sleep, there are subtle changes in your body. When you are coming out of sleep in the morning, there are changes again. One must become aware of them.

When you are going to open your eyes in the morning, do not open them right away. When you have become aware that sleep is over, become aware of your body. Do not open your eyes yet. What is going on? A great change is taking place inside. The sleep is leaving you and the awakening is coming. You have seen the morning sun rising, but never your body rising. It has its own beauty. There is a morning in your body and an evening. It is called *sandhya*: the moment of transformation, the moment of change.

When you are going to sleep, silently watch what is happening. The sleep will come, it will be coming. Be aware! Only then can you become really aware of your physical body. And the moment you become aware of it, you will know what physiological dreaming is. Then in the morning you will be able to remember what was a physiological dream and what was not. If you know the inner feelings, the inner needs, the inner rhythms of your body, then when they are reflected in your dreams you will be able to understand the language.

We have not understood the language of our own bodies. The body has its own wisdom; it has thousands and thousands of years of experience. My body has the experience of my father and mother and their father and mother and so on, centuries and centuries during which the seed of my body has developed into what it is. It has its own language. One must understand it first. When you understand it, you will know what a physiological dream is. And then, in the morning, you can separate the physiological dreams from the nonphysiological dreams.

Only then does a new possibility open up: to be aware of your etheric body. Only then, not before. You become more subtle. You can experience more subtle levels of sounds, perfumes, lights. Then when you walk, you know that the physiological body is walking; the etheric body is not walking. The difference is crystal clear. You are eating. The physical body is eating, not the etheric body. There are etheric thirsts, etheric hungers, etheric longings, but these things can only be seen when the physical body is known completely. Then by and by, the other bodies will become known.

Dreaming is one of the greatest subjects. It is still undiscovered, unknown, hidden. It is part of the secret knowledge. But now the moment has come when everything that is secret must be made open. Everything that was hidden up till now must not be hidden any longer or it may prove dangerous.

In the past it was necessary for some things to remain secret, because knowledge in the hands of ignorance can be dangerous. This is what is happening with scientific knowledge in the West. Now scientists are aware of the crisis and they want to create secret sciences. Nuclear weapons should not have been made known to politicians. Further discoveries must remain unknown. We must wait for the time when man becomes so capable that the knowledge can be made open and it will not be dangerous.

Similarly, in the realm of the spiritual, much was known in the East. But if it fell into the hands of ignorant people it would prove dangerous, so the key was hidden. The knowledge was made secret, esoteric. It was passed on from person to person very guardedly. But now, because of scientific progress, the moment has come for it to be made open. Science will prove dangerous if spiritual, esoteric truths still remain unknown. They must be made open so that spiritual knowledge will be able to keep pace with scientific knowledge.

Dream is one of the greatest esoteric realms. I have said something about it so that you can begin to be aware, but I have not told you the whole science. It is neither necessary nor helpful. I have left gaps. If you go in, these gaps will be filled automatically. What I have said is simply the outer layer. It is not enough for you to be able to make a theory about it, but enough for you to begin.

7

Transcending the Seven Bodies

You said we have seven bodies: an etheric body, a mental body and so on. Sometimes it is difficult to adjust the Indian language to the terms of Western psychology. We have no theory for this in the West, so how can we translate these different bodies into our language? The spiritual is no problem, but the etheric? The astral? The mental? We cannot say this. What can be done?

The words can be translated, but from sources where you haven't looked for them. Jung was better than Freud as far as the search beyond superficial consciousness is concerned, but Jung too is just a beginning. You can get more of a glimpse of what is meant by these things from Steiner's Anthroposophy or from Theosophical writings: Madame Blavatsky's *Secret Doctrine, Isis Unveiled* and other works, or the works of Annie Besant, Leadbeater, Colonel Alcott. You can get a glimpse from Rosicrucian doctrines. There is also a great Hermetic tradition in the West, as well as the secret writings of the Essenes, the Hermetic fraternity by whom Christ was initiated. And more recently, Gurdjieff and Ouspensky can be of help. So something can be found in fragments, and these fragments can be put together.

And what I have said I have said in your terminology. I have used only one word that is not part of Western terminology: the nirvanic. The other six terms—the physical, the etheric, the astral, the mental, the spiritual and the cosmic—are not Indian. They belong to the West as well. In the West the seventh has never been talked about, not because there were no persons who knew about it but because the seventh is impossible to communicate.

If you find these terms difficult, then you can simply use "the first," "the second," "the third" and so on. Don't use any terms to describe them; just describe them. The description will be enough; terminology is of no consequence.

These seven can be approached from so many directions. As far as dream is concerned, Freud's, Jung's and Adler's terms can be used. What they know as the conscious is the first body. The unconscious is the second—not exactly the same, but near enough to it. What they call the collective unconscious is the third—again, not exactly the same but something approximate to it.

And if there are no common terms in usage, new terms can be coined. That is always better in fact, because new terms have no old connotations. When a new term is used, because you have no previous association with it, it becomes more significant and is understood more deeply. So you can coin new words.

The etheric means that which is concerned with the sky and with space. The astral means the minutest, the *sukshma*, the last one, the atomic, beyond which matter ceases to exist. For the mental there are no difficulties. For the spiritual there are no difficulties. For the cosmic too there are no difficulties.

Then you come to the seventh, the nirvanic. Nirvanic means total cessation, the absolute void. Not even the seed exists now; everything has ceased. Linguistically the word means "extinction of the flame." The flame has gone out; the light is turned off. Then you cannot ask where it has gone. It has just ceased to be.

Nirvana means the flame that has gone out. Now it is nowhere, or everywhere. It has no particular point of existence and no particular time or moment of existence. Now it is space itself, time itself. It is existence or nonexistence; it makes no difference. Because it is everywhere, you can use either term. If it is *some*where it cannot be everywhere, and if it is everywhere it cannot be *some*where, so nowhere and everywhere mean the same thing. So for the seventh body you will have to use "nirvanic," because there is no better word for it.

Words in themselves have no meaning at all. Only experiences have meaning. Only if you have experienced something of these seven bodies will it be meaningful to you. To help you, there are different methods to be used on each plane.

Begin from the physical. Then every other step opens for you. The moment you work on the first body, you have glimpses of the second. So begin from the physical. Be aware of it moment to moment. And not only outwardly aware. You can become aware of your body from the inside also. I can become aware of my hand as I have seen it from the outside, but there is an inner feeling to it too. When I close my eyes the hand is not seen, but there is still an inner feeling of something being there. So do not be aware of your body as seen from the outside. This cannot lead you inward. The inner feeling is quite different.

When you feel the body from within, you will know for the first time what it is to be inside the body. When you see it only from the outside you cannot know its secrets. You know only the outer boundaries, how it looks to others. If I see my body from the outside, I see it as it looks to others, but I have not known it *as it is for me*. You can see my hand from the outside and I can see it. It is something objective. You can share the knowledge of it with me. But my hand, looked at in that way, is not known inwardly. It has become public property. You can know it as well as I.

Only the moment I see it from within does it become mine in a way that is unsharable. You cannot know it; you cannot know how I feel it from within. Only *I* can know it. The body that is known to us is not our body. It is the body that is objectively known to all, the body that a physician can know in a laboratory. It is not the body that *is*. Only private, personal knowing can lead you inward; public knowledge cannot. That is why physiology or psychology, which are observations from without, have not led to a knowledge of our inner bodies. It is only the physical body that they know about.

So many dilemmas have been created because of this. One may feel beautiful from within, but we can force him to believe that he is ugly. If we are collectively agreed upon it, he may also come to agree. But no one feels ugly within. The inner feeling is always of beauty.

This outer feeling is not really a feeling at all. It is just a fashion, a criterion imposed from without. A person who is beautiful in one society may be ugly in another; a person who is beautiful in one period of history may not be in another. But the innermost feeling is always of beauty, so if there were no outside criteria there would be no ugliness. We have a fixed image of beauty that everyone shares. That is why there is ugliness and beauty, otherwise not. If we all become blind, no one will be ugly. Everyone will be beautiful.

So the feeling of the body from within is the first step. In different situations the body will feel different from within. When you are in love, you have a particular inner feeling; when you experience hate, the inner feeling is different. If you ask Buddha he will say, "Love is beauty," because in his inner feeling he knows that when he is loving he is beautiful. When there is hatred, anger, jealousy, something happens inwardly that makes you begin to feel ugly. So you will feel yourself to be different in different situations, in different moments, in different states of mind.

When you are feeling lazy, there is a difference from when you are feeling active. When you are sleepy, there is a difference. These differences must be distinctly known. Only then do you become acquainted with the inner life of your body. Then you know the inner history, the inner geography of yourself in childhood, in youth, in old age.

The moment one becomes totally aware of his body from within, the second body automatically comes into view. This second body will be known from the outside now. If you know the first body from the inside, then you will become aware of the second body from the outside.

From outside the first body you can never know the second body, but from inside it you can see the outside of the second body. Every body has two dimensions: the outer and the inner. Just like a wall has two sides—one looking outward and the other looking inward—every body has a boundary, a wall. When you come to know the first body from the inside, you become aware of the second body from the outside.

You are now in between: inside the first body and outside the second. This second body, the etheric body, is like condensed smoke. You can pass through it without any hindrance, but it is not transparent; you cannot look into it from the outside. The first body is solid. The second body is just like the first as far as shape is concerned, but it is not solid.

When the first body dies, the second remains alive for thirteen days. It travels with you. Then, after thirteen days, it too is dead. It disperses, evaporates. If you come to know the second body while the first is still alive, you can be aware of this happening.

The second body can go out of your body. Sometimes in meditation this second body goes up or down, and you have a feeling that gravitation has no pull over you; you have left the earth. But when you open your eyes, you are on the ground, and you know that you were there all the time. This feeling that you have risen comes because of the second body not the first. For the second body there is no gravitation, so the moment you know the second you feel a certain freedom that was unknown to the physical body. Now you can go outside of your body and come back.

This is the second step if you want to know the experiences of your second body. And the method is not difficult. Just wish to be outside your body and you're outside it. The wish itself is the fulfillment. For the second body no effort has to be made because there is no gravitational pull. The difficulty for the first body is because of the gravitational force. If I want to come to your house, I will have to fight with the gravitational force. But if there is no gravitation, then the simple desire will be enough. The thing will happen.

The etheric body is the body that is put to work in hypnosis. The first body is not involved in hypnosis; it is the second body. That is why a person with perfect vision can go blind. If the hypnotist says that you have gone blind, you become blind just by believing it. It is the etheric body that has been influenced; the suggestion goes to the etheric body. If you are in a deep trance, your second body can be influenced. A person who is all right can be paralyzed just by suggesting to him that "you are paralyzed." A hypnotist must not use any language that creates doubt. If he says, "It appears that you have gone blind," it will not work. He must be absolutely certain about it. Only then will the suggestion work.

So in the second body just say: "I am outside the body." Just wish to be outside it, and you will be outside it.

Ordinary sleep belongs to the first body. It is the first body—exhausted by the day's labor, work, tension—relaxing. In hypnosis, it is the second body that is put to sleep. If it is put to sleep, you can work with it.

When you get any disease, seventy-five percent of it comes from the second body and spreads to the first. The second body is so suggestible that first year medical students always catch the same disease that is being studied. They begin to have the symptoms. If headache is being discussed, unknowingly everyone goes inside and begins to ask, "Do I have a headache? Do I have these symptoms?" Because going inward affects the etheric body, the suggestion is caught and a headache is projected, created.

The pain of childbirth is not of the first body; it is of the second. So through hypnosis, childbirth can be made absolutely painless—just by suggestion. There are primitive societies in which women do not feel labor pains because the possibility has never entered their minds. But every type of civilization creates common suggestions that then become part and parcel of everybody's expectations.

Under hypnosis there is no pain. Even surgery can be done under hypnosis without any pain because if the second body gets the suggestion that there will be no pain then there is no pain. As far as I am concerned, every type of pain, and every type of pleasure too, comes from the second body and spreads to the first. So if the suggestion changes, the same thing that has been painful can become pleasurable, and vice versa.

Change the suggestion, change the etheric mind, and everything will be changed. Just wish totally and it will happen. Totality is the only difference between wish and will. When you have wished something totally, completely, with your whole mind, it becomes willpower.

If you wish *totally* to go outside of your physiological body, you can go outside it. Then there is a possibility of knowing the second body from within, otherwise not. When you go outside your physical body, you are no longer in between: inside the first and outside the second. Now you are inside the second. The first body is not.

Now you can become aware of your second body from the inside, just as you became aware of your first body from the inside. Be aware of its inner workings, its inner mechanism, the inner life. The first time you try it is difficult, but after that you will always be within two bodies: the first and the second. Your point of attention will now be in two realms, two dimensions.

The moment you are inside the second body you will be outside the third, the astral. As far as the astral is concerned, there is no need even of any will. Just the wish to be inside is enough. There is no question of totality now. If you want to go in, you can go in. The astral body is a vapor like the second body, but it is transparent. So the moment you are outside, you will be inside. You will not even know whether you are inside or outside because the boundary is transparent.

The astral body is the same size as the first two bodies. Up to the fifth body the size is the same. The content will change, but the size will be the same—up to the fifth. With the sixth body the size will be cosmic. And with the seventh, there will be no size at all—not even the cosmic.

The fourth body is absolutely wall-less. From inside the third body, there is not even a transparent wall. It is just a boundary, wall-less, so there is no difficulty in entering and no need of any method. So one who has achieved the third can achieve the fourth very easily.

But to go beyond the fourth, there is as much difficulty as there was in going beyond the first, because now the mental ceases. The fifth is the spiritual body. Before it can be reached there is again a wall, but not in the same sense as there was a wall between the first body and the second. The wall is between different dimensions now. It is of a different plane.

The four lower bodies were all concerned with one plane. The division was horizontal. Now, it is vertical. So the wall between the fourth and the fifth is bigger than between any two of the lower bodies—because our ordinary way of looking is horizontal, not vertical. We look from side to side, not up and down. But the movement from the fourth body to the fifth is from a lower plane to a higher plane. The difference is not between outside and inside but between up and down. Not unless you begin to look upward can you move into the fifth.

The mind always looks downward. That is why yoga is against the mind. The mind flows downward just like water. Water has never been made the symbol of any spiritual system because its intrinsic nature is to flow downward. Fire has been the symbol of so many systems. Fire goes upward; it never goes downward. So in moving from the fourth body to the fifth body, fire is the symbol. One must look upward; one must stop seeing downward.

How to look upward? What is the way? You must have heard that in meditation the eyes must be looking upward to the *ajna chakra.** The eyes must be focused upward as if you are going to see inside your skull. Eyes are only symbolic. The real question

* The *ajna chakra*, the space between the two eyebrows, is known as the third eye.

is of vision. Our vision, our faculty for seeing, is associated with the eyes, so eyes become the means through which even inward vision happens. If you turn your eyes upward, then your vision too goes upward.

Raja yoga begins with the fourth body. Only *hatha* yoga begins with the first body; other yogas begin from somewhere else. Theosophy begins from the second body, and other systems begin from the third. As civilization goes on progressing to the fourth body, many persons will be able to begin from there. But only if they have worked through the three lower bodies in their past lives can the fourth be used. Those who study *raja* yoga from scriptures or from swamis and gurus without knowing whether or not they have worked through their three lower bodies are bound to be disillusioned because one cannot begin from the fourth. The three must be crossed first. Only then does the fourth come.

The fourth is the last body that it is possible to begin from. There are four yogas; *hatha* yoga for the first body; *mantra* yoga for the second; *bhakti* yoga for the third; and *raja* yoga for the fourth. In ancient days, everybody had to begin with the first body, but now there are so many types of persons: one has worked up to the second body in a previous life, another up to the third, etcetera. But as far as dreaming is concerned, one must begin from the first body. Only then can you know the whole range of it, the whole spectrum of it.

So in the fourth body, your consciousness must become like fire—going upward. There are many ways to check this. For example, if the mind is flowing toward sex it is just like water flowing downward, because the sex center is downward. In the fourth body one must begin directing the eyes up, not down.

If consciousness is to go upward, it must begin from a center that is above the eyes, not below the eyes. There is only one center above the eyes from which the movement can be upward: the *ajna chakra*. Now the two eyes must look upward toward the third eye.

The third eye has been remembered in so many ways. In India, the distinction between a virgin and a girl who is married is made by a color mark on the third eye of the married one. A virgin is bound to look downward toward the sex center, but the moment she is married she must begin to look upward. Sex must change;

she must become a mother. Now her journey is toward nonsexuality—or, beyond sexuality. To help her to remember to look upward, a color mark, a *tika*, is used on the third eye.

Tilak marks have been used on the foreheads of so many types of persons: *sannyasins*, worshipers—so many types of color marks. Or, it is possible to use *chandan* (sandalwood paste). The moment your two eyes look upward toward the third eye, a great fire is created at the center; a burning sensation is there. The third eye is beginning to open and it must be kept cool. So in India, sandalwood paste is used. It is not only cool; it also has a particular perfume that is concerned with the third body and the transcendence of it. The coolness of the perfume, and the particular spot where it is placed, becomes an upward attraction, a remembrance of the third eye.

If you close your eyes and I place my finger at your third eye spot, I am not really touching your third eye itself, but you will still begin to feel it. Even this much pressure is enough. Scarcely a touch, just a gentle fingering. So the perfume, the delicate touch of it and its coolness, is enough. Then your attention is always flowing from your eyes to the third eye.

So to cross the fourth body there is only one technique, one method, and that is to look upward. *Shirshasan* (the headstand), the reverse position of the body, was used as a method to do this because our eyes are ordinarily looking downward. If you stand on your head you will still be looking downward, but now the downward is upward. The flow of your energy downward will be converted into an upward flow.

That is why in meditation, even without knowing it, some persons will go into reverse positions. They will begin to do *shirshasan* because the flow of energy has changed. Their minds are so conditioned to the downward flow that when the energy changes direction they will feel uncomfortable. When they begin to stand on their heads they will feel at ease again, because the flow of energy will again be moving downward. But it will not really be moving downward. In relation to your centers, your *chakras*, the energy will still be moving upward.

So *shirshasan* has been used as a method to take you from the fourth body to the fifth. The main thing to be remembered is to be looking upward. This can be done through *tratak* (staring at a fixed object), through concentration on the sun, through so many different objects. But it is better to do it inwardly. Just close the eyes!

But first, the first four bodies must be crossed. Only then can it be helpful, otherwise not. Otherwise it may be disturbing, it may create all sorts of mental diseases, because the whole adjustment of the system will be shattered. The four bodies are looking downward, and with your inner mind you are looking upward. Then, there is every possibility that schizophrenia will result.

To me, schizophrenia is the result of such a thing. That is why ordinary psychology cannot go deeply into schizophrenia. The schizophrenic mind is simultaneously working in opposite directions: standing outside and looking inside; standing outside and looking upward. Your whole system must be in harmony. If you have not known your physical body from the inside, then your consciousness should be facing downward. That will be healthy; the adjustment is right. You must never try to turn the outward moving mind upward or schizophrenia, division, will be the result.

Our civilizations, our religions, have been the basic cause for humanity's split personality. They have not been concerned with the total harmony. There are teachers who teach methods to move upward to persons who are not even inside their own physical body. The method begins to work and part of the person remains outside his body while a second part moves upward. Then there will be a split between the two. He will become two persons: sometimes this, sometimes that; Jekyll and Hyde.

There is every possibility that a person can become seven people simultaneously. Then the split is complete. He has become seven different energies. One part of him is moving downward, clinging to the first body; another is clinging to the second; another to the third. One part is going upward; another is going somewhere else. He has no center in him at all.

Gurdjieff used to say that such a person is just like a house where the master is absent, and every servant claims he is the master. And no one can deny it, because the master himself is absent. When anybody comes to the house and knocks on the door, the servant who is nearby becomes the master. The next day, another servant answers the door and claims to be the master.

A schizophrenic is without any center. And we are all like that! We have adjusted ourselves to society, that's all. The difference is only of degrees. The master is absent or asleep, and every part of us claims ownership. When the sex urge is there, sex becomes the master. Your mortality, your family, your religion—everything will be denied. Sex becomes the total owner of the house. And then, when sex has gone, frustration follows. Your reason takes charge and says, "I am the master." Now reason will claim the whole house and will deny sex a home.

Everybody claims the house totally. When anger is there, it becomes the master. Now there is no reason, no consciousness. Nothing else can interfere with the anger. Because of this, we cannot understand others. A person who was loving becomes angry and suddenly there is no love. We are at a loss now to understand whether he is loving or not loving. The love was just a servant, and the anger too is just a servant. The master is absent. That is why you cannot ordinarily rely on anybody else. He is not master of himself; any servant can take over. He is no one; he is not a unity.

What I am saying is that one should not experiment with techniques of looking upward before crossing the first four bodies. Otherwise a split will be created which will be impossible to bridge, and one will have to wait for one's next life to begin again. It is better to practice techniques that begin from the beginning. If you have passed your first three bodies in past births, then you will pass them again within a moment. There will be no difficulty. You know the territory; you know the way. In a moment, they come before you. You recognize them—and you have passed them! Then you can go further. So my insistence is always to begin from the first body. For everyone!

To move from the fourth body is the most significant thing. Up to the fourth body you are human. Now you become superhuman. In the first body you are just an animal. Only with the second body does humanity come into being. And only in the fourth does it flower completely. Civilization has never gone beyond the fourth. Beyond the forth is beyond the human. We cannot classify Christ as a human being. A Buddha, a Mahavir, a Krishna, are beyond the human. They are superhuman.

The upward look is a jump from the fourth body. When I am looking at my first body from outside it, I am just an animal with the possibility of being human. The only difference is that I can become human and the animal cannot. As far as the present situation is concerned, we are both below humanity, subhuman. But I have a possibility to go beyond. And from the second body onward, the flowering of the human being happens.

Even someone in the fourth body looks superhuman to us. They are not. An Einstein or a Voltaire looks superhuman, but they are not. They are the complete flowering of the human being and we are *below* human, so they are above us. But they are not above the human. Only a Buddha, a Christ or a Zarathustra is more than human. By looking upward, by raising their consciousness upward from the fourth body, they have crossed the boundary of the mind; they have transcended the mental body.

There are parables worth our understanding. Mohammed, looking upward, says that something has come to him from above. We interpret this *above* geographically, so the sky becomes the abode of the gods. For us, *upward* means the sky; *downward* means the layer below the earth. But if we interpret it in this way, the symbol has not been understood. When Mohammed is looking upward he is not looking toward the sky; he is looking toward the *ajna chakra*. When he says that something has come to him from above, his feeling is right. But, *up* has a different meaning for us.

In every picture, Zarathustra is looking upward. His eyes are never downward. He was looking upward when he first saw the divine. The divine came to him as fire. That is why the Persians have been fire worshippers. This feeling of fire comes from the *ajna chakra*. When you look upward, the spot feels fiery, as if everything is burning. Because of that burning, you are transformed. The lower being is burnt, it ceases to be, and the upper being is born. That is the meaning of "passing through fire."

After the fifth body you move into still another realm, another dimension. From the first body to the fourth body the movement is from outside to inside; from the fourth to the fifth it is from downward to upward; from the fifth it is from ego to nonego. Now the dimension is different. There is no question of outside, inside, upward or downward. The question is of "I" and "non-I." The question is now concerned with whether there is a center or not.

A person is without any center up to the fifth—split in different parts. Only for the fifth body is there a center: a unity, oneness. But the center becomes the ego. Now this center will be a hindrance for further progress. Every step that was a help becomes a hindrance for further progress. You have to leave every bridge you cross. It was helpful in crossing, but it will become a hindrance if you cling to it.

Up to the fifth body, a center has to be created. Gurdjieff says this fifth center is the crystallization. Now there are no servants; the master has taken charge. Now the master is the master. He is awakened; he has come back. When the master is present, the servants subside; they become silent.

So when you enter the fifth body, crystallization of the ego happens. But now, for further progress, this crystallization must be lost again. Lost into the void, into the cosmic. Only one who *has* can lose, so to talk about egolessness before the fifth body is nonsense, absurd. You do not have an ego, so how can you lose it? Or you can say that you have many egos, every servant has an ego. You are multi-egoistic, a multi-personality, a multi-psyche, but not a unified ego.

You cannot lose the ego because you do not have it. A rich man can renounce his riches, but not a poor one. He has nothing to renounce, nothing to lose. But there are poor people who think about renunciation. A rich person is afraid of renunciation because he has something to lose, but a poor one is always ready to renounce. He is ready, but he has nothing to renounce.

The fifth body is the richest. It is the culmination of all that is possible for a human being. The fifth is the peak of individuality, the peak of love, of compassion, of everything that is worthwhile. The thorns have been lost. Now, the flower too must be lost. Then there will simply be perfume, no flower.

The sixth is the realm of perfume, cosmic perfume. No flower, no center. A circumference, but no center. You can say that everything has become a center, or that now there is no center. Just a diffused feeling is there. There is no split, no division—not even the division of the individual into the "I" and the "non-I," the "I" and "the other." There is no division at all.

So the individual can be lost in either of two ways: one, schizophrenic, splitting into many subpersons; and another, cosmic—lost into the ultimate; lost into the greater, the greatest, the Brahma; lost into the expanse. Now the flower is not, but the perfume is.

The flower too is a disturbance, but when only the perfume is, it is perfect. Now there is no source, so it cannot die. It is undying. Everything that has a source will die, but now the flower is not, so there is no source. The perfume is uncaused, so there is no death and no boundary to it. A flower has limitations; perfume is unlimited. There is no barrier to it. It goes on and on, and goes beyond.

So from the fifth body the question is not of upward, downward, sideways, inside, outside. The question is whether to be with an ego or without an ego. And the ego is the most difficult thing of all to lose. The ego is not a problem up to the fifth body because progress is ego-fulfilling. No one wants to be schizophrenic; everyone would prefer to have a crystallized personality. So every *sadhaka*, every seeker, can progress to the fifth body.

There is no method to move beyond the fifth body because every type of method is bound with the ego. The moment you use a method, the ego is strengthened. So those who are concerned with going beyond the fifth, talk of no-method. They talk of methodlessness, of no-technique. Now there is no *how*. From the fifth, there is no method possible.

You can use a method up to the fifth, but then no method will be of use because the *user* is to be lost. If you use anything, the user will become stronger. His ego will go on crystallizing; it will become a nucleus of crystallization. That is why those who have remained in the fifth body say there are infinite souls, infinite spirits. They think of each spirit as if it were an atom. Two atoms cannot meet. They are windowless, doorless; closed to everything outside themselves.

Ego is windowless. You can use a word of Leibnitz: *monads*. Those who remain in the fifth body become monads: windowless atoms. Now you are alone, and alone, and alone.

But this crystallized ego has to be lost. How to lose it when there is no method? How to go beyond it when there is no path? How to escape from it? There is no door. Zen monks talk about the gateless gate. Now there is no gate, and still one has to go beyond it.

So what to do? The first thing: do not be identified with this crystallization. Just be aware of this closed house of "I." Just be aware of it—don't do anything—and there is an explosion! You will be beyond it.

They have a parable in Zen. A goose egg is put in a bottle. The goose comes out of the egg and begins to grow, but the mouth of the bottle is so small that the goose cannot come out of the bottle. It grows bigger and bigger, and the bottle becomes too small to live in. Now, either the bottle will have to be destroyed to save the goose, or the goose will die. Seekers are asked: "What is to be done? We do not want to lose either. The goose is to be saved and the bottle also. So what to do?" This is the question of the fifth body. When there is no way out and the goose is growing, when the crystallization has become consolidated, what to do now?

The seeker goes inside a room, closes the door and begins to puzzle over it. What to do? Only two things seem to be possible: either to destroy the bottle and save the goose, or to let the goose die and save the bottle. The meditator goes on thinking and thinking. He thinks of something, but then it will be cancelled because there is no way to do it. The teacher sends him back to think some more.

For many nights and many days the seeker goes on thinking, but there is no way to do it. Finally a moment comes when thinking ceases. He runs out shouting, "Eureka! The goose is out!" The teacher never asks how, because the whole thing is just nonsense.

So to move from the fifth body, the problem becomes a Zen *koan*. One should just be aware of the crystallization—and the goose is out! A moment comes when you are out; there is no "I." The crystallization has been gained and lost. For the fifth, crystallization (the center, the ego) was essential. As a passage, as a bridge, it was a necessity; otherwise the fifth body could not be crossed. But now it is no longer needed.

There are persons who have achieved the fifth without passing through the fourth. A person who has many riches has achieved the fifth; he has crystallized in a way. A person who has become president of a country has crystallized in a way. A Hitler, a Mussolini, are crystallized in a way. But the crystallization is in the fifth body. If the four lower bodies are not in accordance with it, then the crystallization becomes a disease. Mahavir and Buddha are crystallized too, but their crystallization is different.

We all long to fulfill the ego because of an innermost need to reach the fifth body. But if we choose a shortcut, then in the end we will be lost. The shortest way is through riches, power, politics.

The ego can be achieved, but it is a false crystallization; it is not in accordance with your total personality. It is like a corn that forms on your foot and becomes crystallized. It is a false crystallization, an abnormal growth, a disease.

If the goose is out in the fifth, you are in the sixth. From the fifth to the sixth is the realm of mystery. Up to the fifth, scientific methods can be used, so yoga is helpful. But after that it is meaningless, because yoga is a methodology, a scientific technique.

In the fifth, Zen is very helpful. It is a method to go from the fifth to the sixth. Zen flowered in Japan but it began in India. Its roots came from yoga. Yoga flowered into Zen.

Zen has had much appeal in the West because the Western ego is, in a sense, crystallized. In the West, they are the masters of the world; they have everything. But the ego has become crystallized through the wrong process. It has not developed through the transcendence of the first four bodies. So Zen has become appealing to the West but it will not help because the crystallization is wrong. Gurdjieff is much more helpful to the West because he works from the first body to the fifth. He is not helpful beyond the fifth. Only up to the fifth, to the crystallization. Through his techniques, you can achieve a proper crystallization.

Zen has been just a fad in the West because it has no roots there. It developed through a very long process in the East, beginning with *hatha* yoga and culminating in the Buddha. Thousands and thousands of years of humbleness: not of ego but of passivity; not of positive action but of receptivity—through a long duration of the female mind, the receptive mind. The East has always been female, while the West is male: aggressive, positive. The East has been an openness, a receptivity. Zen could be of help in the East because other methods, other systems, worked on the four lower bodies. These four became the roots, and Zen could flower.

Today, Zen has become almost meaningless in Japan. The reason is that Japan has become absolutely Western. Once the Japanese were the most humble people, but now their humbleness is just a show. It is no longer part of their innnermost core. So Zen has been uprooted in Japan and is popular now in the West. But this popularity is only because of the false crystallization of the ego.

From the fifth body to the sixth, Zen is very helpful. But only then, neither before nor beyond. It is absolutely useless for the other bodies, even harmful. To teach university level courses in the primary school not only does not help; it may be harmful.

If Zen is used before the fifth body you may experience *satori*, but that is not *samadhi.** Satori is a false *samadhi*. It is a glimpse of *samadhi*, but it is just a glimse. As far as the fourth body (the mental body) is concerned, *satori* will make you more artistic, more aesthetic. It will create a sense of beauty in you; it will create a feeling of well-being. But it will not be a help in crystallization. It will not help you to move from the fourth body to the fifth.

Only beyond crystallization is Zen helpful. The goose is out of the bottle, without any *how*. But only at this point can it be practiced, after so many other methods have been used. A painter can paint with closed eyes; he can paint as if it is a game. An actor can act as if he is not acting. In fact, the acting becomes perfect only when it does not look like acting. But many years of labor have gone into it, many years of practice. Now the actor is completely at ease, but that at-easeness is not achieved in a day. It has its own methods.

We walk, but we never know how we do it. If someone asks you how you walk you say, "I just walk. There is no *how* to it." But the *how* takes place when a child begins to walk. He learns. If you were to tell the child that walking needs no method—"You just walk!"—it would be nonsense. The child would not understand it. Krishnamurti has been talking this way, talking with adults who have children's minds, saying, "You can walk. You just walk!" People listen. They are charmed. Easy! To walk without any method. Then, everyone can walk.

Krishnamurti too has become attractive in the West, and just because of this. If you look at *hatha* yoga or *mantra* yoga or *bhakti* yoga or *raja* yoga or *tantra*, it looks so long, so arduous, so difficult. Centuries of labor are needed, births and births. They cannot wait. Some shortcut, something instantaneous must be there. So Krishnamurti appeals to them. He says, "You just walk. You walk into God. There is no method." But no-method is the most arduous thing to achieve. To act as if one is not acting, to

* For a more complete description of the difference between *satori* and *samadhi*, see the chapter on this subject in *Meditation: The Art of Ecstasy*, Bhagwan Shree Rajneesh, Harper & Row, New York, 1976.

speak as if one is not speaking, to walk effortlessly as if one is not walking, is based on long effort.

Labor and effort are necessary; they are needed. But they have a limitation. They are needed up to the fifth body, but they are useless from the fifth to the sixth. You will go nowhere; the goose will never be out.

That is the problem with Indian yogis. They find it difficult to cross the fifth because they are method-enchanted, method-hypnotized. They have always worked with method. There has been a clear-cut science up to the fifth and they progressed with ease. It was an effort—and they could do it! No matter how much intensity was needed, it was no problem to them. No matter how much effort, they could supply it. But now in the fifth, they have to cross from the realm of method to no-method. Now they are at a loss. They sit down, they stop. And for so many seekers, the fifth becomes the end.

That is why there is talk of five bodies, not seven. Those who have gone only to the fifth think that it is the end. It is not the end; it is a new beginning. Now one must move from the individual to the nonindividual. Zen, or methods like Zen, done effortlessly, can be helpful.

Zazen means just sitting, doing nothing. A person who has done much cannot conceive of this. Just sitting and doing nothing! It is inconceivable. A Gandhi cannot conceive of it. He says, "I will spin my wheel. Something must be done. This is my prayer, my meditation." Nondoing to him means doing nothing. Nondoing has its own realm, its own bliss, its own adjustment, but that is from the fifth body to the sixth. It cannot be understood before that.

From the sixth to the seventh, there is not even no-method. Method is lost in the fifth, and no-method is lost in the sixth. One day you simply find that you are in the seventh. Even the cosmos has gone; only nothingness is. It just happens. It is a happening from the sixth to the seventh. Uncaused, unknown.

Only when it is uncaused does it become discontinuous with what went before. If it is caused then there is a continuity and the being cannot be lost—even in the seventh. The seventh is total nonbeing: nirvana, emptiness, nonexistence.

There is no possibility of any continuity in moving from existence to nonexistence. It is just a jump, uncaused. If it were caused there would be a continuity, and it would be just like the sixth body. So to move from the sixth body to the seventh cannot even be talked about. It is a discontinuity, a gap. Something was, and something now is—and there is no connection between the two. Something has just ceased, and something has just come in. There is no relationship between them. It is as if a guest has left from one door and another guest has entered from the other side. There is no relationship between the going of one and the coming of the other. They are unrelated.

The seventh body is the ultimate, because now you have crossed even the world of causation. You have gone to the original source, to that which was before creation and that which will be after annihilation. So from the sixth to the seventh there is not even no-method. Nothing is of any help; everything can be a hindrance. From the cosmic to nothingness there is just a happening: uncaused, unprepared for, unasked for.

It happens instanteously. Only one thing is to be remembered: you must not cling to the sixth. Clinging will prevent you from moving to the seventh. There is no positive way to move to the seventh, but there can be a negative hindrance. You can cling to the Brahma, the cosmos. You can say, "I have reached!" Those who say they have reached cannot go to the seventh.

Those who say, "I have known," remain in the sixth. So those who wrote the Vedas remained in the sixth. Only a Buddha crosses the sixth because he says, "I do not know." He refuses to give answers to the ultimate questions. He says, "No one knows. No one has known." Buddha could not be understood. Those who heard him said, "No, our teachers have known. They say Brahma is." But Buddha is talking of the seventh body. No teacher can say he has known about the seventh because the moment you say it you lose touch with it. Once you have known it, you cannot say. Up to the sixth body symbols can be expressive, but there is no symbol for the seventh. It is just an emptiness.

There is a temple in China that is totally empty. There is nothing in it: no image, no scriptures, nothing. It is just bare, naked walls. Even the priest resides outside. He says, "A priest can only be outside the temple; he cannot be inside." If you ask the priest where the deity of the temple is, he will say, "See it!"—and there is emptiness; there is no one. He will say, "See! Here! Now!" and there is only a naked, bare, empty temple.

If you look for objects then you cannot cross the sixth to the seventh. So there are negative preparations. A negative mind is needed, a mind that is not longing for anything—not even *moksha*, not even deliverance, not even nirvana, not even truth; a mind that is not waiting for anything—not even for God, for Brahma. It just *is*, without any longing, without any desire, without any wish. Just is-ness. Then, it happens . . . and even the cosmos is gone.

So you can cross into the seventh by and by. Begin from the physical and work through the etheric. Then the astral, the mental, the spiritual. Up to the fifth you can work and then, from the fifth on, just be aware. Doing is not important then; consciousness is important. And finally, from the sixth to the seventh, even consciousness is not important. Only is-ness, being. This is the potentiality of our seeds. This is our possibility.

8

Becoming and Being

Please tell us something about the tensions and relaxation of the seven bodies.

The original source of all tension is becoming. One is always trying to be something; no one is at ease with himself as he is. The being is not accepted, the being is denied, and something else is taken as an ideal to become. So the basic tension is always between that which you are and that which you long to become.

You desire to become something. Tension means that you are not pleased with what you are, and you long to be what you are not. Tension is created between these two. What you desire to become is irrelevant. If you want to become wealthy, famous, powerful, or even if you want to be free, liberated, to be divine, immortal, even if you long for salvation, *moksha*, then too the tension will be there.

Anything that is desired as something to be fulfilled in the future, against you *as you are*, creates tension. The more impossible the ideal is, the more tension there is bound to be. So a person who is a materialist is ordinarily not so tense as one who is religious, because the religious person is longing for the impossible, for the far-off. The distance is so great that only a great tension can fill the gap.

Tension means a gap between what you are and what you want to be. If the gap is great, the tension will be great. If the gap is small, the tension will be small. And if there is no gap at all, it means you are satisfied with what you are. In other words, you do not long to be anything other than what you are. Then your mind exists in the moment. There is nothing to be tense about; you are at ease with yourself. You are in the Tao. To me, if there is no gap you are religious; you are in the *dharma*.*

* The law of nature, the universal spiritual law.

The gap can have many layers. If the longing is physical, the tension will be physical. When you seek a particular body, a particular shape—if you long for something other than what you are on a physical level—then there is tension in your physical body. One wants to be more beautiful. Now your body becomes tense. This tension begins at your first body, the physiological, but if it is insistent, constant, it may go deeper and spread to the other layers of your being.

If you are longing for psychic powers, then the tension begins at the psychic level and spreads. The spreading is just like when you throw a stone in the lake. It drops at a particular point, but the vibrations created by it will go on spreading into the infinite. So tension may start from any one of your seven bodies, but the original source is always the same: the gap between a state that is and a state that is longed for.

If you have a particular type of mind and you want to change it, transform it—if you want to be more clever, more intelligent—then tension is created. Only if we accept ourselves totally is there no tension. This total acceptance is the miracle, the only miracle. To find a person who has accepted himself totally is the only surprising thing.

Existence itself is nontense. Tension is always because of hypothetical, nonexistential possibilities. In the present there is no tension; tension is always future-oriented. It comes from the imagination. You can imagine yourself as something other than you are. This potential that has been imagined will create tension. So the more imaginative a person is, the more tension is a possibility. Then the imagination has become destructive.

Imagination can also become constructive, creative. If your whole capacity to imagine is focused in the present, in the moment, not in the future, then you can begin to see your existence as poetry. Your imagination is not creating a longing; it is being used in living. This living in the present is beyond tension.

Animals are not tense, trees are not tense, because they do not have the capacity to imagine. They are below tension, not beyond it. Their tension is just a potentiality; it has not become actual. They are evolving. A moment will come when tension will explode in their beings and they will begin to long for the future. It is bound to happen. The imagination becomes active.

The first thing the imagination becomes active about is the

future. You create images and because there are no corresponding realities, you go on creating more and more images. But as far as the present is concerned, you cannot ordinarily conceive of the imagination in relation to it. How can you be imaginative in the present? There seems to be no need. This point must be understood.

If you can be *consciously present* in the present, you will not be living in your imagination. Then the imagination will be free to create within the present itself. Only the right focus is needed. If the imagination is focused on the real, it begins to create. The creation may take any form. If you are a poet, it becomes an explosion of poetry. The poetry will not be a longing for the future, but an expression of the present. Or if you are a painter, the explosion will be of painting. The painting will not be of something as you have imagined it, but as you have known it and lived it.

When you are not living in the imagination, the present moment is given to you. You can express it, or you can go into silence. But the silence, now, is not a dead silence that is practiced. This silence too is an expression of the present moment. The moment is so deep that now it can be expressed only through silence. Not even poetry is adequate; painting is not adequate. No expression is possible. Silence is the only expression. This silence is not something negative but, rather, a positive flowering. Something has flowered within you, the flower of silence, and through this silence all that you are living is expressed.

A second point is also to be understood. This expression of the present through the imagination is neither an imagination of the future nor a reaction against the past. It is not an expression of any experience that has been known. It is the experience of experiencing—as you are living it, as it is happening in you. Not a lived experience, but a living process of experiencing.

Then your experience and experiencing are not two things. They are one and the same. Then there is no painter. The experiencing itself has become the painting; the experiencing itself has expressed itself. You are not a creator. You are creativity, a living energy. You are not a poet; you are poetry. The experience is neither for the future nor for the past; it is neither *from* the future nor *from* the past. The moment itself has become eternity, and everything comes from it. It is a flowering.

This flowering will have seven layers, just like tension has seven layers. It will exist in every body. For example, if it happens on the physiological level, you will become beautiful in quite a new sense. This beauty is not of form but of the formless, not of the visible but of the invisible. And if you can feel this nontense moment in your body, you will know a well-being that you have not known before, a positive well-being.

We have known states of well-being that are negative: negative in the sense that when we are not ill we say we are healthy. This health is simply a negation of disease. It has nothing positive about it; it is just that disease is not there. The medical definition of health is that if you are not ill then you are healthy. But health has a positive dimension also. It is not just the absence of illness; it is the presence of health.

Your body can be nontense only when you are living a moment-to-moment existence. If you are eating and the moment has become eternity, then there is no past and no future. The very process of eating is all that is. You are not doing something; you have become the doing. There will be no tension; your body will feel fulfilled. Or if you are in sexual communion and the sex is not just a relief from sexual tension but, rather, a positive expression of love—if the moment has become total, whole, and you are in it completely—then you will know a positive well-being in your body.

If you are running, and the running has become the totality of your existence; if you *are* the sensations that are coming to you, not something apart from them but one with them; if there is no future, no goal to this running, running itself is the goal—then you know a positive well-being. Then your body is nontense. On the physiological level, you have known a moment of nontense living.

And the same is true with each of the seven bodies. To understand a nontense moment in the first body is easy because we already know two things that are possible in the body: disease (a positive illness) and a negatively defined well-being (an absence of illness). This much we have already known, so we can conceive of a third possibility, that of positive well-being (health). But to understand what nontension is in the second body, the etheric, is a bit more difficult, because you have not known anything about it. But still, certain things can be understood.

Dreams are basically concerned with the second body, the etheric. So ordinarily when we talk about dreams what we are talking about are dreams of the etheric body. But if your physical body has been living in tension, then many dreams will be created by it. For example, if you have been hungry or on a fast, then a particular type of dream is created. This is physiological dreaming. It is not concerned with the etheric body.

The etheric body has its own tension. We know the etheric body only in dreams, so if the etheric body is tense, the dream becomes a nightmare. Even in your dream you will be tense now; the tension will follow you.

The first tension in the etheric body is concerned with the fulfillment of your desires. We all have dreams about love. Sex is physiological; love is not. Love has nothing to do with the physical body, it is concerned with the etheric body; but if it is not fulfilled, then even your physical body may suffer because of it. Not only does your physical body have needs that have to be fulfilled, but your etheric body also has needs. It has its own hungers; it also needs food. Love is that food.

We all go on dreaming about love, but we are never in love. Everybody dreams about love—how it should be, with whom it should be—and everyone is frustrated in it. Either we are dreaming about the future or, in frustration, about the past; but we are never loving.

There are other tensions in the etheric body as well, but love is the one that can be most easily understood. If you can love *in the moment*, then a nontense situation is created in the etheric body. But you cannot love in the moment if you have demands, expectations, conditions for your love, because demands, expectations and conditions are concerned with the future.

The present is beyond our specifications. It is as it is. But you can have expectations about the future: how it *should* be. Love too has become a "should"; it is always about what "should be." You can be loving in the present only if your love is not an expectation, a demand, only if it is unconditional.

Also, if you are loving only to one person and not to someone else, then you can never love in the present. If your love is a relationship and not a state of mind, you cannot love in the present because, very subtly, that too is a condition. If I say I can be loving only to you, then when you are not there I will not be loving. For twenty-three hours I will be in a state of not-loving and only for one hour, when I am with you, will I be loving. This is impossible! You cannot be in a state of love one moment and not be in love another moment.

If I am healthy, I am healthy for twenty-four hours. It is impossible to be healthy for one hour and unhealthy for the other twenty-three hours. Health is not a relationship; it is a state of being.

Love is not a relationship between two persons. It is a state of mind within yourself. If you are loving, you are loving to everybody. And not only to persons; to things as well. Love moves from you to objects also. Even when you are alone, when no one is there, you are loving. It is just like breathing. If I take an oath that I will breathe only when I am with you, only death can follow. Breathing is not relationship; it is not tied to any relationship. And for the etheric body, love is just like breathing. It is its breath.

So either you are loving, or you are not loving. The type of love that humanity has created is very dangerous. Even disease has not created as much nonsense as this so-called love has created. The whole humanity is diseased because of this wrong notion of love.

If you can love and be loving, irrespective of whom, then your second body can have a sense of well-being, a positive at-easeness. Then there are no nightmares. Dreams become a poetry. Then something happens in your second body, and the perfume of it not only pervades you but others also. Wherever you are, the perfume of your love spreads. And of course it has its own response, its own echoing.

Real love is not a function of the ego. The ego is always asking for power, so even when you love—because your love is not real, because it is just a part of the ego—it is bound to be violent. Whenever we love it is a violence, a type of war. Father and son, mother and daughter, husband and wife—they are not lovers; we have converted them into enemies. They are constantly fighting, and only when they are not fighting do we say it is love. The definition is negative. Between two battles there is a gap, a period of peace.

But really, between two wars there is no possibility of peace. The so-called peace is only a preparation for the coming war. There is no peace between husband and wife, no love. The gap that we call love is only a preparation for the coming fight. We think that there is health when we are between two illnesses, and we think that there is love when we are between two fights. It is not love. It is only a gap between fights. You cannot go on fighting for twenty-four hours, so at some point you begin to love your enemy.

Love is never possible as a relationship but only as a state of mind. If love comes to you as a state of mind, then your second body (the etheric body) becomes at ease, nontense. It is relaxed. There are other reasons for tension in the second body, but I am talking about the one that can be most easily understood. Because we think we know love, it can be talked about.

The third body is the astral body. It has its own tensions. They are concerned not only with this life but with your previous lives. Tension in the third body is because of the accumulation of everything you have been and of everything you have been longing for. Your total longing, thousands and thousands of lives and their repetitive longings, are in the astral body. And you have always been longing! It does not matter for what. The longing is there.

The astral body is a storehouse of your total longings, your total desires. That is why it is the most tense part of your being. When you go into meditation you become aware of astral tensions, because meditation starts from the third body. People who have begun to be aware of these tensions through meditation come to me and say, "Since I started meditating, tensions have increased." They have not increased, but you have become aware of them now. Now you know something that you were not aware of before.

These are astral tensions. Because they are essences of so many lives, they cannot be described by any particular word. Nothing can be said about them that can be understood. They can only be lived, and known.

Desiring itself is the tension. We are never without the desire for something or other. There are even people who desire desirelessness. It becomes a total absurdity. In the third body, the astral body, you can desire to be desireless. In fact, the desire to be desireless is one of the strongest desires. It can create one of the biggest gaps between what is and what you want to be.

So accept your desires as they are, and know that you have had so many desires throughout so many lives. You have desired so much, and the whole thing has been accumulated. So for the third body (the astral body), accept your desires as they are. Do not fight with them; do not create a desire against desires. Just accept them. Know that you are full of desires, and be at ease with it. Then you will become nontense in the astral body.

If you can accept the infinite crowd of desires within you without creating a desire *against* these desires; if you can be in the crowd of desires (they are your whole accumulated past) and accept them as they are; if this acceptance becomes a total—then, in a single moment, the whole crowd disappears. They are no longer there, because they can exist only against a background of desiring, a constant desiring for that which is not.

The object of desire does not matter; it is irrelevant. Desire even desirelessness and the background is there; the whole crowd will be there. If you accept your desire, a moment of desirelessness is created. You accept your desire as it is. Now there is nothing to desire; desiring is not there. You accept everything as it is, even your desires. Then the desires evaporate; nothing has to be done with them. The astral body becomes at ease; it comes to a state of positive well-being. Only then can you proceed to the fourth body.

The fourth body is the mental body. Just as there are desires in the astral body, in the mental body there are thoughts: contradictory thoughts, a whole crowd of them, each thought asserting itself as the whole, each thought possessing you as if it were the whole. So the tension in the fourth body is created by thoughts. Being without thoughts—not asleep, not unconscious, but a thoughtless consciousness—is the health, the well-being of the fourth body. But how can one be conscious and thoughtless?

Every moment, new thoughts are being created. Every moment something of your past is coming into conflict with something of your present. You were a communist and now you are a Catholic and believe in something else, but the past is still there. You can become a Catholic, but you cannot throw off your communism. It remains in you. You can change your thoughts, but the discarded thoughts are always there waiting. You cannot unlearn them. They reach into your depths; they go into the unconscious. They will not show themselves to you because you have discarded them, but they will remain there, waiting for their chance. And the chance will come. Even in a period of twenty-four hours, there will be a moment when you will be a communist again and then again you will be a Catholic. This will go on and on, back and forth, and the total effect will be confusion.

So for the mental body, tension means confusion—contradictory thoughts, contradictory experiences, contradictory expectations—and ultimately results in a confused mind. And the confused mind will only become more confused if it tries to go beyond confusion, because out of a state of confusion, no-confusion cannot be achieved.

You are confused. Spiritual seeking will create a new dimension for your confusion. All your other confusions are still there, and now a new confusion has been added. You meet this guru, then that, then the next, and each guru brings new confusion to you. The old confusion will be there, and a new one will be added. You will be a madhouse. This is what happens in the fourth body, the mental body. There, confusion is the tension.

How can one cease to be confused? You can cease to be confused only if you do not deny one particular thought in favor of another, if you do not deny anything—if you do not deny communism in favor of religiousness, if you do not deny God in favor of a philosophy of atheism. If you accept everything that you think, there is no choice to be made and tensions disappear. If you go on choosing, you go on adding to your tensions.

Awareness must be choiceless. You must be aware of your total thought process, the total confusion. The moment you become aware of it, you will know that it is all confusion. Nothing is to be chosen; the whole house must be discarded. Once you know it is just a confusion, the house can be discarded at any time; there is no difficulty in discarding it.

So begin to be aware of your total mind. Do not choose; be choiceless. Do not say, "I am an atheist," or, "I am a theist." Do not say, "I am a Christian," or, "I am a Hindu." Do not choose. Just be aware that sometimes you are an atheist and sometimes a theist, sometimes you are a Christian and sometimes a communist, sometimes a saint and sometimes a sinner. Sometimes one ideology appeals to you and sometimes another, but these are all fads.

Be totally aware of it. The very moment you become aware of the total process of your mind is a moment of nonidentity. Then you are not identified with your mind. For the first time you know yourself as consciousness and not as mind. Mind itself becomes an object to you. Just as you are aware of other people, just as you are aware of the furniture in your house, you become aware of your mind, the mental process. Now you are this awareness—unidentified with the mind.

The difficulty with the fourth body, the mental body, is that we are identified with our minds. If your body becomes ill and someone says you are ill, you do not feel offended; but if your mind becomes ill and someone says, "Your mind is ill; you seem to be going insane," then you are offended. Why?

When someone says, "Your body seems to be ill," you feel that he has sympathized with you. But if someone says something about mental illness—that as far as your mind is concerned, you seem to be derailed; you are neurotic—then you are offended because there is a deeper identification with the mind than with the body.

You can feel yourself to be separate from the body. You can say, "This is my hand." But you cannot say, "This is my mind," because you think: "My mind means me." If I want to operate on your body you will allow me, but you will not allow me to operate on your mind. You will say, "No, this is too much! My freedom will be lost!" Mind is much more deeply identified. It is us. We do not know anything beyond it, so we are identified with it.

We know something beyond the body: the mind. That is why the possibility of being nonidentified with the body exists. But we do not know anything beyond the mind. Only if you become aware of thoughts can you come to know that mind is nothing but a process, an accumulation: a mechanism, a storehouse, a computer of your past experiences, your past learning, your past knowledge. It is not you; you can be without it. The mind can be operated on. It can be changed; it can be thrown from you.

And now, new possibilities are there. Someday even your mind will be able to be transplanted into someone else. Just as the heart can be transplanted, sooner or later memory will be able to be transplanted. Then a person who is dying will not die completely. At least his memory can be saved and transplanted into a new child. The child will acquire the whole memory of the person. He will talk about experiences through which he has not passed but he will say, "I have known." Whatever the dead man knew the child will know, because the whole mind of the dead person has been given to him.

This seems dangerous, and it is possible that we will not allow it to happen because our own identity will be lost. We are our minds! But to me, the possibility has much potentiality. A new humanity may be born out of it.

We can be aware of the mind because the mind is not us; it is not "me." My mind is as much a part of my body as my kidney is. Just as I can be given a new kidney and I will still be the same person, with nothing changed, so too I can go on living with a transplanted mind with nothing changed. I can go on being the old self I was, but with a new mind added to me. Mind too is a mechanism. But because of our identification with it, tension is created.

So with the fourth body, awareness is health and unawareness is disease; awareness is nontension and nonawareness is tension. Because of thoughts, because of your identification with them, you go on living in your thoughts and a barrier is created between you and your existential being.

There is a flower within your reach, but you will never come to know it because you are thinking about it. The flower will die, and you will go on thinking about it. Thinking has created a film between you and the experience—transparent, but not *so* transparent; only an illusion of transparency.

For example, you are listening to me. But it may be that you are not really listening. If you are thinking about what I am saying, you have ceased listening. Then you have gone ahead or gone back; you are not with me. Either it is the past you will be repeating in your mind or it will be the future projected through the past, but it will not be what I am saying.

It is even possible that you can repeat verbatim what I have said. Your mechanism is recording it. It can repeat what I have said, reproduce it. Then you will claim, "If I have not heard you, how can I reproduce it?" But a tape recorder does not hear me. Your mind can go on working just like a machine. You may be present, or you may not be. You are not needed. You can go on thinking and still be listening. The mind—the fourth body, the mental body—has become a barrier.

Between you and that-which-is there is a barrier. The moment you come to touch, you move away from the experience. The moment you come to look, you move away. I take your hand in my hand. This is an existential thing. But it may be that you are not there. Then you have missed. You have known—you have touched and experienced—but you were in your thoughts.

So at the fourth body one must be aware of one's thought process, taken as a whole. Not choosing, not deciding, not judging; just aware of it. If you become aware, you become nonidentified. And nonidentification with the mechanism of the mind is non-tension.

The fifth body is the spiritual body. As far as the spiritual body is concerned, ignorance of oneself is the only tension. All the time you *are*, you know perfectly well that you do not know yourself. You will pass through life, you will do this and that, you will achieve this and that, but the sense of self-ignorance will be with you continuously. It will be lurking behind you; it will be a constant companion no matter how much you try to forget it, how much you try to escape from it. You cannot escape from your ignorance. You *know* that you don't know. This is the disease at the fifth level.

Those in Delphi who wrote on the temple, "Know thyself," were concerned with the fifth body. They were working on it. Socrates continuously repeated: "Know thyself." He was concerned with the fifth body. For the fifth body, *atma gyana* (self-knowledge) is the only knowledge.

Mahavir said, "By knowing oneself, one knows all." It is not so. One cannot know all by knowing oneself. But the antithesis is correct. By not knowing oneself, one cannot know anything. So to balance this, Mahavir said, "By knowing yourself, you will know all." Even if I know everything, if I do not know myself, what is the use? How can I know the basic, the foundational, the ultimate, if I have not even known myself? It is impossible.

So with the fifth body, the tension is between knowing and ignorance. But remember, I am saying "knowing and ignorance"; I am not saying "knowledge and ignorance." Knowledge can be gathered from scriptures; knowing cannot be gathered from anywhere. There are so many persons operating under this fallacy, this misunderstanding between knowledge and knowing. Knowing is always yours. I cannot transfer my knowing to you; I can only transfer my knowledge. Scriptures communicate knowledge, not knowing. It can say you are divine, you are *atman*, you are the Self, but this is not knowing.

If you cling to this knowledge, great tension will be there. Ignorance will be there along with false, acquired knowledge and information—borrowed knowledge. You will be ignorant, but you will feel that you know. Then there is much tension. It is better to be ignorant and know perfectly that "I am an ignorant man." Then tension is there, but it is not so great. If you do not delude yourself with knowledge acquired from others, then you can seek and search within yourself, and knowing is possible.

Because you *are*, this much is certain: that whatever you are, you *are*. This cannot be denied. Another thing: you are someone who knows. It may be that you know others, it may be that you know only illusions, it may be that what you know is not correct, but you know. So two things can be taken for granted: your existence and your consciousness.

But a third thing is lacking. The essential personality of man can be conceived through three dimensions: existence, consciousness and bliss—*sat/chit/anand*. We know that we are existence itself; we know that we are someone who knows—consciousness itself. Only the bliss is lacking. But if you seek inside yourself, you will know the third also. It is there. The blissfulness, the ecstasy of one's existence is there. And when you know it, you will know yourself completely: your existence, your consciousness, your bliss.

You cannot know yourself completely unless bliss is known, because a person who is not blissful will go on escaping from himself. Our whole life is an escape from ourselves. Others are significant to us because they help us to escape. That is why we are all other-oriented. Even if one becomes religious, he creates God as the other. He becomes other-oriented again; the same fallacy is repeated.

So at the fifth stage, one has to be in search of oneself from within. This is not a search, but a "being in search."

Only up to the fifth body are you needed. Beyond the fifth, things become easy and spontaneous.

The sixth body is cosmic. The tension is between you—your feelings of individuality, of limitation—and the unlimited cosmos. Even in the fifth stage you will be embodied in your spiritual body. You will be a person. That "person" will be the tension for the sixth. So to achieve a nontense existence with the cosmos, to be in tune with the cosmos, you must cease to be an individual.

Jesus says, "Whoever loses himself will find himself." This statement is concerned with the sixth body. Up to the fifth it cannot be understood, because it is completely antimathematical. But from the sixth, this is the only mathematics, the only rational possibility: to lose oneself.

We have been enhancing ourselves, crystallizing ourselves. Up to the fifth body the crystallization, the selfhood, the individuality can be carried; but if someone insists on being an individual, he remains with the fifth. So many spiritual systems stop with the fifth. All those who say that the soul has its own individuality, and the individuality will remain even in a liberated state—that you will be an individual, embodied in your selfhood—any system that says this, stops with the fifth. In such a system, there will be no concept of God. It is not needed.

The concept of God comes only with the sixth body. "God" means the cosmic individuality, or, it would be better to say, the cosmic no-individuality. It is not that "I" am in existence; it is the total within me that has made it possible for me to exist. I am just a point, one link among infinite links of existence. If the sun does not rise tomorrow, I will not be. I will go out of existence; the flame will go out. I am here because the sun exists. It is so far away, but still it is linked with me. If the earth dies, as so many planets have died, then I cannot live because my life is one with the life of the earth. Everything exists in a chain of existence. It is not that we are islands. We are the ocean.

At the sixth, the feeling of individuality is the only tension against an oceanic feeling—a feeling without limitation, a feeling that is beginningless and endless, a feeling not of *me* but of *we*. And the "we" includes everything. Not only persons, not only organic beings, but everything that exists. "We" means the existence itself.

So "I" will be the tension at the sixth. How can you lose the "I," how can you lose your ego? You will not be able to understand right now, but if you achieve the fifth, it will become easy. It is just like a child who is attached to a toy and cannot conceive of how he can throw it. But the moment childhood is gone, the toy is thrown. He never goes back to it. Up to the fifth body the ego is very significant, but beyond the fifth it becomes just like a toy that a child has been playing with. You just throw it; there is no difficulty.

The only difficulty will be if you have achieved the fifth body as a gradual process and, not as a sudden enlightenment. Then, to throw the "I" completely in the sixth becomes difficult. So beyond the fifth, all those processes that are sudden become helpful. Before the fifth, gradual processes seem to be easier; but beyond the fifth, they become a hindrance.

So at the sixth, the tension is between individuality and an oceanic consciousness. The drop must lose itself to become the ocean. It is not really losing itself, but from the standpoint of the drop it seems so. On the contrary, the moment the drop is lost, the ocean has been gained. It is not really that the drop has lost itself. It has become the ocean now.

The seventh body is the nirvanic. The tension in the seventh body is between existence and nonexistence. In the sixth, the seeker has lost *himself*, but not existence. He *is*—not as an individual, but as the cosmic being. Existence is there. There are philosophies and systems that stop with the sixth. They stop with God or with *moksha* (liberation). The seventh means to lose even existence into nonexistence. It is not losing oneself. It is just losing. The existential becomes nonexistential. Then you come to the original source from which all existence comes and into which it goes. Existence comes out of it; nonexistence goes back into it.

Existence itself is just a phase. It must go back. Just as day comes and night follows, just as night goes and day follows, so existence comes and nonexistence follows; nonexistence comes and existence follows. If one is to know totally, then he must not escape from nonexistence. If he is to know the total circle, he must become nonexistential.

Even the cosmic is not total, because nonexistence is beyond it. So even God is not total. God is just part of Brahma; God is not Brahman itself. Brahman means all light and darkness combined, life and death combined, existence and nonexistence combined. God is not death; God is only life. God is not nonexistence; God is only existence. God is not darkness; God is only light. He is only *part* of the total being, not the total.

To know the total is to become nothing. Only nothingness can know the wholeness. Wholeness is nothingness, and nothingness is the only wholeness—for the seventh body.

So these are the tensions in the seven bodies, beginning with the physiological. If you understand your physiological tension, the relief of it and the well-being of it, then you can very easily proceed to all seven bodies. The realization of at-easeness in the first body becomes a stepping stone to the second. And if you realize something in the second—if you feel a nontense etheric moment—then the step toward the third is taken. In each body, if you start with well-being, the door to the next body opens automatically. But if you are defeated in the first body it becomes very difficult, even impossible, to open up further doors.

So begin with the first body and do not think of the other six bodies at all. Live in the physical body completely, and you will suddenly know that a new door has opened. Then continue on further. But never think of the other bodies or it will be disturbing and will create tensions.

So whatever I have said—forget it!

9

The Fallacy of Knowledge

Bhagwan, what do you teach and what is your doctrine?

I am not teaching a doctrine. Teaching a doctrine is rather meaningless. I am not a philosopher; my mind is antiphilosophical. Philosophy has led nowhere and cannot lead anywhere. The mind that thinks, that questions, cannot know.

There are so many doctrines. But a doctrine is a fiction, a human fiction. It is not a discovery but an invention. The human mind is capable of creating infinite systems and doctrines, but to know the truth through theories is impossible. A mind that is stuffed with knowledge is a mind that is bound to remain ignorant.

Revelation comes the moment knowledge ceases. There are two possibilities: either we can think about something, or we can go into it existentially. The more a person thinks, the more he moves away from what is here and now. To think about something is to lose contact with it.

So what I teach is an antidoctrinaire, antiphilosophical, antispeculative experience. How to be, just to *be*. How to be in the moment that is here and now. Open, vulnerable, one with it. That is what I call meditation.

Knowledge can only lead to fiction, to projecting things. It cannot be a vehicle for the attainment of truth. But once you have known the truth, knowledge can be a vehicle to communicate, to share with someone who doesn't know. Then language, doctrines, theories can become a means. But it is still not adequate. It is bound to falsify.

Anything that has been known existentially cannot be expressed totally. You can only indicate it. The moment I express what I have known, the word goes to you but the meaning is left behind. A dead word comes to you. In a way it is meaningless, because the meaning was the experience itself.

So knowledge can become a vehicle of expression, but not a means toward the achievement of realization. The knowing mind is a hindrance, because when you know you are not humble. When you are stuffed with knowledge there is no space within you to receive the unknown. The mind must become vacant, void: a womb, a total receptivity.

Knowledge is your past. It is what you have known. It is your memory, your accumulation, your possession. The accumulation becomes a barrier. It comes between you and the new, between you and the unknown.

You can be open to the unknown only when you are humble. One must constantly be aware of one's ignorance: that there is still something unknown. A mind that is based on memories, information, scriptures, theories, doctrines, dogmas, is egocentric not humble. Knowledge cannot give you humbleness. Only the vast unknown can make you humble.

So memory must cease. It is not that you should be without memory, but that in the moment of knowing, in the moment of experiencing, memory must not be there. In that moment, an open, vulnerable mind is required. This moment of emptiness, of void, is meditation, *dhyana*.

Won't the experience itself become a doctrine?

The experience can only be communicated to others negatively. I cannot say what it is, but I can say what it is not. Language can be a vehicle to express what it is not. When I say language cannot express it, I am still expressing it. When I say no doctrine about it is possible, that is my doctrine. But this is negative. I am not asserting something; I am denying something. The *no* can be said; the *yes* cannot be said. The *yes* must be realized.

If there is a lingering belief in knowledge, it will become a hindrance in achieving the void, in achieving meditation. First one must understand the futility of the past, of the known, of the knowledge of the mind. As far as the unknown is concerned, as far as truth is concerned, such knowledge is futile.

Either you can become identified with what you have known, or you can become a witness to it. If you become identified with it, then you and your memory become one. But if there is no identification—if you have remained aloof from your memories, separate, not identified with them—then you are aware of yourself as something different from your memories. This awareness becomes a path toward the unknown.

The more you are able to be a witness to your knowledge (the less you identify yourself as the knower), the less possibility there is of your ego becoming the possessor of this knowledge. If you are different from your memories, then the memories become just a sort of accumulated dust. They have come through experience and have become part and parcel of your mind, but your consciousness is different. The one who remembers is different from that which is remembered; the one who has known is different from that which has been known. If you are clear about this distinction, you come nearer and nearer to the void. Nonidentified, you can be open; you can be without memories coming between you and the unknown.

The void can be achieved, but it cannot be created. If you create it, it is bound to be created by your old mind, by your knowledge. That is why there can be no method to achieve it. A method can come only from your accumulated information, so if you try to use any method it is bound to be a continuity of your old mind. But the unknown cannot come to you as a continuity. It can come only as a discontinuous gap. Only then is it beyond the known, beyond your knowledge.

So there can be no method as such, no methodology; only the understanding that "I am separate from that which I have accumulated." If this is understood, then there is no need of cultivating the void. The thing has happened! You *are* the emptiness! Now there is no need to create it.

One cannot create the void. A created void will not be the void; it will only be your creation. Your creation can never be nothingness, the void, because it will have boundaries. You have created it, so it cannot be more than you; it cannot be more than the mind that has created it. You cannot create the void; it must enter you. You can only be a receiver of it. And you can be prepared to receive it only in a negative way. Prepared in the sense that you must not be identified with your knowledge; prepared in the sense that you have understood the futility, the meaninglessness of everything you have known.

Only this awareness of the thinking process can throw you into a gap where that-which-is overwhelms you, where that-which-is is always present. Now there is no barrier between you and it. You have become one with the moment, one with eternity, with the infinite.

The moment one translates this moment into knowledge, it again becomes part and parcel of the memory. Then it is lost. So one can never say, "I have known." The unknown remains unknown. However much one may have experienced it, the unknown still remains to be known. The charm of it, the beauty of it, the attraction of it remains the same.

The process of knowing is eternal, so one can never come to a point when he can say, "I have reached." If someone says this, he again falls into the pattern of memory, the pattern of knowledge. Then he becomes dead. The moment knowledge is asserted is the moment of death. Life ceases. Life is always *from* the unknown, *toward* the unknown. It comes from the beyond and goes toward the beyond. So to me, a religious person is not a person who claims knowledge. A person who claims knowledge may be a theologian, a philosopher, but never a religious person. A religious mind accepts the ultimate mystery, the ultimate unknowableness, the ultimate ecstasy of ignorance, the ultimate bliss of ignorance.

The moment of meditation, of emptiness, cannot be created; it cannot be projected. You cannot *make* your mind still. If you do, then either you have intoxicated it or you have hypnotized it, but this is not the void. The void comes. It can never be created; it can never be brought.

So I am not teaching any method. In the sense that there are methods, techniques, doctrines, I am not a teacher.

You have convinced me. How can I transform this conviction into an experience?

There is no *how*, because *how* implies a method. There is only an awakening. If you are listening to me and something awakens within you, then the experience will happen to you; you will feel something. I am not trying to convince you. An intellectual conviction is no conviction at all. I am just conveying a fact to you.

Why are you convinced by what I have said? There are two possibilities: either you have been convinced by my argument, or you see the truth in what I've said as a fact in yourself. If my argument becomes a conviction then you will ask *how*, but if what I am saying is experienced by you, if you realize it to be true within yourself, that knowledge is separate from me. I am not providing you with any knowledge. Rather, the experience itself is happening while I'm talking.

When the intellect is convinced, it asks: how? What is the way? It wants to know. But I am not giving you any doctrine. I am just telling you my experience. When I say that memory is an accumulation—that it is dead, it is just a hangover from the past—what I mean is that it is a part of the past that is clinging to you, but you are separate from it. If the feeling of what I mean comes to you, and you have a glimpse of the distance between you and your memory (your consciousness and your memory), then there is no *how*. Something has happened, and this something can go on penetrating you from moment to moment—not through any method, but through your awareness, your constant remembrance.

Now you know that consciousness is different from the contents of consciousness. If this becomes a moment-to-moment awareness—while you are walking, talking, eating, sleeping—then something happens. If you are constantly aware that the mind is just a computerized, built-in process to accumulate memories and not a part of your being, then this awareness alone, this no-method alone, will help this *something* to happen within you.

No one can say when it will happen, how it will happen, where it will happen, but if awareness continues, by itself it becomes deeper and deeper. It is an automatic process. From the intellect it goes to the heart; from the intelligence it goes to your intuitive mind; from the conscious it moves slowly to the unconscious. And one day, you become totally awakened. Something has happened. Not as a cultivation, but as a by-product of remembering. Not by the cultivation of any doctrine, but because you have awakened to an inner fact, an inner vision. Something has gone deep in you.

When the moment comes, it comes completely unprecedented, unknown—as an explosion. In that moment of explosion, you are completely empty. You are *not*; you cease to be. There is no intellect, no reason, no memory. There is simply consciousness: consciousness of nothingness, of the void. In that void is knowledge. But it is knowledge in quite another sense. Now there is no knower and no known. There is simply knowing. It is existential.

What exists in the void, what the void is, cannot be communicated. Only the passage, the process, can be communicated. But the process cannot be conceived of as a method; it is not something to be practiced. There is nothing to practice. Either you *remember*, or you do not.

Do you recommend any particular way of living as a preparation?

The moment you become aware, your whole life, your whole way of living will change. But these changes will come to you; they should not be practiced. The moment you practice something, it loses whatever is significant in it. So whatever changes come about should happen spontaneously.

There is no question of anything being practiced. The question is simply to understand that you cannot desire the void. It is not just a contradiction in terms, but an existential contradiction. You cannot desire it because the very desire comes from your old mind, from your knowledge. All that you can do is to be aware of what you are. The moment you become aware of yourself as you are, a separation occurs, a division, a partition. A part of you becomes unidentified with the rest of you.

Then there are two: I and me. The "me" is the memory, the mind; and the "I" is the consciousness, the *atman*.

You must listen to me, and simultaneously listen to your inner mind. This process should go on all the time. What I am saying is becoming a part of your "me," a part of your accumulation, a part of your knowledge. This knowledge will ask for further knowledge—about the *how*, the method. And if some method is shown, that too will become part of your knowledge. Your "me" will be strengthened; it will become more knowledgeable.

My emphasis is not on your "me"; I am not talking to your "me." If your "me" comes in, then the communication does not become a communion. Then it is simply a discussion, not a dialogue. It becomes a dialogue only if there is no "me." If you are here but your "me" is not here, then there is no question of *how*. What I am saying will either be seen as a truth or as an untruth, either as a fact or as a hocus-pocus doctrine.

My concern is just to create a situation—either by talking, or by silence, or by confusing you. My aim is to create a situation where your "I" comes outside of you, your "I" comes beyond your "me." I try to create so many situations.

This too is a kind of situation. I am saying absurd things to you. I am talking about achieving something, and still denying any method. This is absurd! How can I be saying something and still say that it cannot be said? But it is absurdity itself that can create the situation. If I convince you, it will not create the situation. It will become part of your "me," part of your knowledge. Your "me" goes on asking: how? What is the way? I will deny the way and still talk of the transformation. Then the situation becomes so irrational that your mind is not satisfied. Only then can something from beyond take over.

All the time I am creating situations. For intellectual people, absurdity must be the situation. Awareness comes only when a situation is created where the continuity is disrupted. The very absurdity and unreasonableness of the situation must create a gap, shattering and disturbing the individual to the point of awareness.

I am reminded of an incident in the life of Buddha. One morning he came to a village. As he entered the village, someone said to him, "I am a believer in the Supreme. Please tell me whether God is."

Buddha denied it absolutely. He said, "There is no God. There never has been and there never will be. What nonsense you are saying!" The man was shattered, but the situation was created.

In the afternoon, another man came to Buddha and said, "I am an atheist. I do not believe in God. Is there a God? What do you say about it?"

Buddha said, "Only God is. Nothing exists except him." The man was shattered.

Then in the evening, a third man came to Buddha and said, "I am an agnostic. I neither believe nor disbelieve. What do you say? Is there a God or not?"

Buddha remained silent. The man was shattered.

But a certain monk, Anand, who always accompanied Buddha, was shattered even more. In the morning Buddha had said, "There is no God," in the afternoon he had said, "Only God is," and in the evening he had remained silent. That night Anand said to Buddha, "Before you go to sleep, please answer my question. You have shattered my peace! I am at a loss! What do you mean by these absurd, contradictory answers?"

Buddha said, "None of them was given to you. Why have you listened to them? Those answers were each given to the person who asked. If the answers have disturbed you, good. That is your answer."

So situations can be created. A Zen monk creates situations in his own way. He may push you out of his room, or slap you on your face. It looks absurd. You ask one thing, and he answers about something else. Someone asks, "What is the Way?" but the Zen monk's answer is not concerned with the Way at all. He may say, "See the river!" or "See that tree! How tall it is!" This is absurd.

The mind seeks continuity. It is afraid of absurdities. It is afraid of the nonrational, of the unknown. But truth is not a by-product of intellectualization. It is neither a deduction nor an induction. It is not logical; it is not a conclusion.

I am not conveying anything to you. I am just creating a situation. If the situation is created, then something that cannot be conveyed is conveyed. So do not ask *how*. Just be. Be aware if you can, and if you cannot, then be aware of your unawareness. Be attentive to what is. If you cannot, then be attentive to your inattention. And the thing will happen. The thing happens.

By "creating an absurd situation," do you mean that a person must be disturbed in some way? What will be the result?

People are disturbed enough already. But because they are disturbed already, they have identified themselves with their disturbances. They have become at ease with them. The disturbances have become habitual. We are disturbed already! It is impossible to be undisturbed and not know the truth.

Disturbance is our normal situation, so when I disturb you, *your disturbance is disturbed*. Then the disturbance is negated. You become calm for the first time. When I talk about creating an absurd situation, it is not to achieve any result but only as a means to convey a message that is essentially nonconveyable.

You ask, "What will be the result?" Something can be said about it provided that what is said is not taken to be the truth. It should be taken only in a symbolic, poetic, mythical sense. To me, every religious scripture is a myth and every assertion that comes from a person who has gone through the happening is, in a sense, untrue. It is not the truth but only an indicator. The indicator has to be forgotten before the truth can be known.

There are three words that indicate the boundary beyond which there is only silence. These words are *sat/chit/anand*: existence, consciousness, bliss. The experience is one, but when we make a concept of it we divide it into these three phases. It is always experienced as one but conceptualized as these three.

In this total existence (*sat*), this total is-ness, you alone are. You are neither this nor that; you are not identified with anything. There is simply is-ness.

The second is consciousness (*chit*). This does not mean the conscious mind. The conscious mind is only a fragment of a greater unconscious one. Ordinarily when we are conscious we are conscious of something. The consciousness is objective; it is about something. *Chit* is pure consciousness, consciousness of nothing. There is no object. The consciousness is not directed toward anything; it is undirected. It is infinite, pure.

The last is *anand*, bliss. Not happiness, not joy, but bliss. Happiness includes a state of unhappiness—a remembrance of it, a contrast to it. Joy too has a certain tension about it, something that has to be released, that has to subside. Bliss is happiness without any trace of unhappiness; it is joy without any abyss around it. It is happiness without any tension.

Bliss is the midpoint between joy, at one extreme, and sorrow at the other. It is the midpoint, the point of transcendence. It has the depth of sorrow and the height of joy, both. Joy has height but no depth, while sorrow has depth, an abyssmal depth, but no peak. Bliss has both the height of joy and the depth of sorrow, so it transcends both. Only the midpoint can be a total transcendence of the two extremes.

These three terms, *sat/chit/anand*, are the boundary: the most that can be said and the least of what can be experienced. This is the last thing that can be expressed and the boundary from which one can jump into the inexpressible. This is not the end. It is only the beginning.

Satchitanand is only an expression, not the reality. If this is remembered, then no harm will be done. But the mind forgets, and then the expression *satchitanand* becomes a reality. We form theories around it, doctrines, and the mind becomes closed. Then there is no jump. This has happened in India. The whole tradition has been woven around these three words. But reality is not *satchitanand*; it is beyond it. This is only as much of it as can be put into words. It should be taken as a metaphor. All religious literature is a parable; it is symbolic. It is a verbalization of what is intrinsically inexpressible.

I don't even like to use the term *satchitanand* because the moment the mind knows what is to happen it begins to ask and demand. Then it demands *satchitanand*, and teachers come along who supply the demand with *mantras*, with techniques, with methods. Every demand can be supplied, so a nonsensical demand will be supplied with absurdities. All theologies and all gurudoms are created in this way.

One has to be aware all the time not to make the ultimate into a goal to be desired. Do not make it a wish, or an object to be achieved, or a destination to travel to. It is right here now! If we can become aware, the explosion can happen. It's already nearby, it's our closest neighbor, but we go on desiring the far off. It's beside us, and we go on a long pilgrimage. It follows us like a shadow, but we never see it because our eyes are far away in the distance.

Life must be in the being. There is a saying of Lao Tzu: "Seek, and you will lose. Do not seek, and find."

10

Windows to the Divine

In Indian philosophy, the nature of ultimate truth has been described as truth (satyam), *beauty* (sundaram) *and goodness* (shivam). *Are these the characteristics of God?*

These are not the qualities of God. Rather, they are our experiences of God. They do not belong to the divine as such; they are our perceptions. The divine, by itself, is unknowable. Either it is every quality, or no quality at all. But as the human mind is constituted, it can experience the divine through three windows: you can have the glimpse either through beauty or through truth or through goodness.

These three dimensions belong to the human mind. They are our limitations. The frame is given by us; the divine itself is frameless. It is like this. We can see the sky through the window. The window looks like a frame around the sky, but the sky itself has no frame around it. It is infinite. Only the window gives it a frame. In the same way, beauty, truth and goodness are the windows through which we can glance into the divine.

Human personality is divided into three layers. If intellect is predominant, then the divine takes the shape of truth. The intellectual approach creates the window of truth, the frame of truth. If the mind is emotional—if one comes to reality not through the head but through the heart—then the divine becomes beauty. The poetic quality is given by you. It is only the frame. Intellect gives it the frame of truth; emotion gives it the frame of beauty. And if the personality is neither emotional nor intellectual—if action is predominant—then the frame becomes goodness.

So here in India we use these three terms for the divine. *Bhakti* yoga means the way of devotion and is for the emotional type. God is seen as beauty. *Jnana* yoga is the way of knowledge. God is seen as truth. And *karma* yoga is the way of action. God is goodness.

The very word "God" comes from the word "good." This word has had the greatest influence because most of humanity is predominantly active, not intellectual or emotional. This does not mean that there is no intellect or emotion, but they are not predominant factors. Very few are intellectual and very few are emotional. The majority of humanity is predominantly active. Through action, God becomes "the good."

But the opposite pole must exist too, so if God is perceived as the good then the devil will be perceived as the bad. The active mind will perceive the devil as the bad; the emotional mind will perceive the devil as the ugly; and the intellectual mind will perceive the devil as the untrue, the illusory, the false.

These three characteristics (truth, goodness and beauty) are human categories framed around the divine, which is, in itself, frameless. They are not qualities of the divine as such. If the human mind can perceive the divine through any fourth dimension, then this fourth dimension will also become a quality of the divine. I don't mean that the divine is not the good. I'm only saying that this goodness is a quality that is chosen by us and seen by us. If man did not exist in the world then the divine would not be good, the divine would not be beautiful, the divine would not be true. Divinity would exist all the same, but these qualities, which are chosen by us, would not be there. These are just human perceptions. We can perceive the divine to be other qualities as well.

We do not know if animals perceive the divine, we do not know how they perceive things at all, but one thing is certain: they will not perceive the divine in human terms. If they perceive the divine at all, they will feel and perceive it in quite a different way from us. The qualities they perceive will not be the same as they are for us.

When a person is predominantly intellectual, he cannot conceive of how you can say God is beautiful. The very concept is absolutely foreign to his mind. And a poet cannot conceive that truth can mean anything except beauty. It cannot mean anything else to him. Truth is beauty; all else is simply intellectual. For a poet, for a painter, for a man who perceives the world in terms of the heart, truth is a naked thing without beauty. It is just an intellectual category.

So if a particular mind is predominantly intellectual, it cannot understand the emotional mind, and vice versa. That is why there is so much misunderstanding and so many definitions. No single definition can be accepted by the whole humanity. God must come to you in your own terms. When you define God, you will be part of the definition. The definition will come from you; God as such is indefinable. So those who look at him through these three windows have, in a way, imposed themselves, their own definitions, on the divine.

There is also the possibility of a fourth way of seeing the divine for one who has transcended these three divisions in his personality. In India, we do not have a word for the fourth. We simply call it *turiya* (the fourth). There is a type of consciousness where you are neither intellectual nor emotional nor active, but just conscious. Then you are not looking at the sky through any window. You have come out of your house and you know the windowless sky. There is no pattern, no frame.

Only the type of consciousness that has realized the fourth can understand the limitations of the other three. It can understand the difficulty of understanding among the others, and can also understand the underlying similarities among beauty, truth and goodness. Only the fourth type can understand and tolerate. The other three types will always be quarreling.

All religions belong to one of these three categories. And they have been constantly quarreling. Buddha cannot take part in this conflict. He belongs to the fourth type. He says, "It is all nonsense. You are not quarreling about divine qualities; you are quarreling about your windows. The sky remains the same from any window."

So these are not divine qualities. These are divine qualities *as perceived by us*! If we can destroy our windows, we can know the divine as qualityless, *nirguna*. Then we go beyond qualities. Only then does human projection not come in.

But then it becomes very difficult to say anything. Whatever can be said about the divine can be said only through the windows, because anything that can be said is really being said about the windows, not about the sky itself. When we see beyond the windows, the sky is so vast, so limitless. It cannot be defined. All words are inapplicable; all theories are inadequate.

So one who is in the fourth has always remained silent about it, and definitions of the divine have come from the first three. If the one in the fourth has spoken at all, he has spoken in terms that seem absurd, illogical, irrational. He contradicts himself. Through contradiction he tries to show something. Not to say something; to show something.

Wittgenstein has made this distinction. He said that there are truths that can be said, and there are truths that can be shown but not said. A thing is definable because it exists among other things. It can be related to other things, compared. For example, we can always say that a table is not a chair. We can define it by reference to something else. It has a boundary to which it extends, and beyond which something else begins. Really, only the boundary is defined. A definition means the boundary from which everything else begins.

But we cannot say anything about the divine. The divine is the total, so there is no boundary; there is no frontier from which something else begins. There is no "something else." The divine is frontierless so it cannot be defined.

The fourth can only show; it can only indicate. That is why the fourth has remained mysterious. And the fourth is the most authentic, because it is not colored by human perceptions. All the great saints have indicated; they have not said anything. Whether it is Jesus, Buddha, Mahavir or Krishna, it doesn't matter. They are not saying anything; they are just indicating something—just a finger pointing to the moon.

But there is always the difficulty that you will become obsessed by the finger. The finger is meaningless; it is indicating something else. It must not catch your eye. If you want to see the moon, the finger must be absolutely forgotten.

This has been the greatest difficulty as far as the divine is concerned. You see the indication and you feel that this indication is, itself, the truth. Then the whole purpose is destroyed. The finger is not the moon; they are absolutely different. The moon can be shown by the finger, but one must not cling to the finger. If a Christian cannot forget the Bible, if a Hindu cannot forget the Gita, then the very purpose is destroyed. The whole thing becomes purposeless, meaningless and in a way nonreligious, antireligious.

Whenever one approaches the divine, one must be aware of one's own mind. If one approaches the divine through the mind, the divine becomes colored by it. If you approach the divine without mind, without you, without the human coming in; if you approach the divine as an emptiness, as a void, a nothingness; without any preconceptions, without any propensity for seeing things in a particular way—then you know the qualitylessness of the divine, otherwise not. Otherwise all the qualities we give to the divine belong to our human windows. We impose them upon the divine.

Are you saying that we do not need to use the window to see the sky?

Yes. It is better to look from the window than not to look at all, but to look through the window cannot be compared to the windowless sky.

But how does one get from the room to the sky without the window?

You can pass through the window to go to the sky, but you must not remain at the window. Otherwise the window will always be there. The window must be left behind. It must be passed through and transcended.

Once one is in the sky there are no words—until one comes back into the room. Then the story comes. . . .

Yes, one can come back. But then he cannot be the same as he was before. He has known the patternless, the infinite. Then even from the window he knows that the sky is not patterned, not windowed. Even from behind the window he cannot be deceived. Even if the window is closed and the room becomes dark, he knows that the infinite sky is there. Now he cannot be the same again.

Once you have known the infinite, you have *become* the infinite. We are what we have known, what we have felt. Once you have known the boundless, the boundaryless, in a way you have become infinite. To know something is to be that. To know love is to be love; to know prayer is to be prayer; to know the divine is to be the divine. Knowing is realization; knowing is being.

Do all three windows become one?

No. Each window will remain as it was. The window has not changed; *you* have changed. If the person is emotional he will go out and come in through that window, but now he will not deny other windows; he will not be antagonistic to them. Now he will be understanding of the others. He will know that other windows also lead to the same sky.

Once you have been under the sky, you know that the other windows are part of the same house. Now you may wander to other windows or you may not. It depends on you. You need not; one window is enough. If a person is like Ramakrishna he may wander to other windows to see whether the same sky is seen through them. It depends on the person. One may look through other windows or one may not.

And really, there is no need. To know the sky is enough. But one may inquire, be curious. Then he will look through other windows. There have been persons who have wandered and persons who have not. But once a person has known the open sky, he will not deny other windows; he will not deny other approaches. He will confirm that their windows open to the same thing. So a person who has known the sky becomes religious, not sectarian. The sectarian mind remains behind the window; the religious mind is beyond it.

One who has seen the sky may wander; he may go to other windows also. There are infinite windows. These are the main types, but they are not the only windows. There are so many combinations possible.

Is there a window for every consciousness, for each man?

Yes. In a way each person comes to the divine from his own window. And each window is basically different from any other. Infinite are the windows, infinite are the sects. Each person has a sect of his own. Two Christians are not the same. One Christian differs from another as much as Christianity differs from Hinduism.

Once you have come to the sky, you know that all differences belong to the house. They never belong to you. They belong to the house in which you lived, through which you saw, through which you felt, but not to you as such.

When you come under the sky, you know that you were also part of the sky—only living within walls. The sky within the house is not different from the sky beyond the house. Once we come out we know that the barriers were not real. Even a wall is not a barrier to the sky; it has not divided the sky at all. It creates an appearance that the sky is divided—that this is my house and that house is yours; that the sky in my house belongs to me and the sky in your house belongs to you—but once you have come to know the sky itself, there is no difference. Then there are no individuals as such. Then waves are lost and only the ocean remains. You will come back inside again, but now you will not be different from the sky.

It seems there are so few Christians who have gone to the sky and who have come back with this concept.

There are some. Saint Francis, Eckhart, Böhme. . . .

They didn't tell us it was the same sky, did they?

They could not. The sky is always the same, but they cannot report on the sky in the same way. Reports about the sky are bound to be different, but what is being reported is not different.

To those who have not known the reported thing itself, the report will be everything. Then the differences become acute. But all that is reported is just a selection, a choice. The whole cannot be reported; only a part of the whole can be reported. And when it is reported, it becomes dead.

Saint Francis can report only as a Saint Francis can report. He cannot report like Mohammed, because the report does not come from the sky. The report comes from the pattern, from the individuality. It comes from the mind: the memory, the education, the experiences; from the words, the language, the sect; from the living. The report comes from all that. It is not possible for the communication to come only from Saint Francis, because a report can never be individual. It must be communal or it will be an absolute failure.

If I report in my own individual language, no one will understand it. When I experienced the sky, I experienced it without the community. I was totally alone at the moment of knowing. There was no language; there were no words. But when I report, I report to others who have not known. I must speak in their language. I will have to use a language that was known to me prior to my knowing.

Saint Francis uses the Christian language. As far as I am concerned, religions are only different languages. To me, Christianity is a particular language derived from Jesus Christ. Hinduism is another language; Buddhism is another language. The difference is always of language. But if one knows only the language and not the experience itself, the difference is bound to be vast.

Jesus said "the kingdom of God" because he was speaking in terms that could be understood by his audience. The word "kingdom" was understood by some and misunderstood by others. The cross followed; crucifixion followed. Those who understood Jesus understood what was meant by "the kingdom of God," but those who could not understand thought that he was dealing with a kingdom on earth.

But Jesus could not use Buddha's words. Buddha would never have used the word "kingdom." There are so many reasons for the difference. Jesus came from a poor family; his language was that of a poor man. To a poor man the word "kingdom" is very expressive, but to Buddha there was nothing significant about the word because Buddha himself had been a prince. The word was meaningless for Buddha, but meaningful for Jesus.

Buddha became a beggar and Jesus became a king. That is bound to be. The other pole becomes meaningful. The unknown pole becomes expressive of the unknown. For Buddha, begging was the most unknown thing, so he took the form of the unknown, the form of a beggar. For him, *bhikkhu* (beggar) became the most significant term.

The word *bhikkhu* is never used in India because there are so many beggars here. Instead, we use the word swami (master). When someone becomes a *sannyasin*, when he renounces, he becomes a swami, a master. But when Buddha renounced he became a *bhikkhu*, a beggar. For Buddha, this word carried something that it could not carry for Jesus.

Jesus could only speak in terms that were borrowed from Jewish culture. He could change something here and there, but he could not change the total language or no one would have been able to understand. So in a sense, he was not a Christian. By the time Saint Francis came along, a Christian culture had developed with its own language. So Saint Francis was more of a Christian than Christ himself. Christ remained a Jew; his whole life was Jewish. It could not be otherwise.

If you are born a Christian, then Christianity may not be expressive to you; it may not touch you. The more you have known it, the more it becomes meaningless. The mystery is lost. To a Christian, the Hindu attitude may be more meaningful, more significant. Because it is unknown, it can be expressive of the unknowable.

As far as I am concerned, it is better that a person not remain with the religion of his birth. The attitudes and beliefs that were given to him at birth must be denied sometime or the adventure will never begin. One should not remain where one was born. One should go to unknown corners and feel the exhilaration of it.

Sometimes we cannot understand the very thing that we think we have understood the most. A Christian thinks that he understands Christianity. That becomes the barrier. A Buddhist thinks he understands Buddhism because he knows it, but this very sense of knowing becomes a hindrance. Only the unknown can become the magnetic, the occult, the esoteric.

One must transcend the circumstances of one's birth. It is just circumstantial that one is a Christian by birth; it is just circumstantial that one is a Hindu by birth. One should not be confined to the conditions of his birth. One must be twice-born as far as religion is concerned. One must go to the unknown corners. Then the thrill is there. The exploration begins.

Religions are, in a way, complementary. They must work for others; they must accept others. A Christian or a Hindu or a Jew must know the thrill of conversion. The thrill of conversion creates the background for transformation. Whenever someone comes from the West to the East there is something new. The Eastern attitude is so different that it cannot be put into familiar categories. The whole attitude is so opposite to what you are familiar with that if you want to understand it, you yourself will have to change.

The same thing happens to someone from the East when he goes to the West. It *should* happen. One should be open so it can happen. It is the unknown, the unfamiliar, that will create a change.

In India, we could not create a religion like Christianity. We could not create a theology. We could not create the Vatican, the Church. There are temples, but there is no Church. The Eastern mind is basically illogical so it is bound to be chaotic in a sense. It is bound to be individual; it cannot be organizational.

A Catholic priest is something very different. He is trained to be part of an organization. He belongs somewhere in the hierarchy. And it works. An establishment, a hierarchy is logical, so Christianity has been able to be spread throughout the world.

Hinduism has never tried to convert anybody. Even if someone has converted himself, Hinduism is not at ease with him. It is a nonconverting religion, nonorganizational. There is no priesthood in the sense that exists in Catholicism. The Hindu monk is just a wandering individual—without any hierarchy, without belonging to any establishment. He is absolutely rootless. As far as the outside world is concerned this approach is bound to be a failure, but as far as the individual is concerned, as far as the inner depth is concerned, it is bound to be a success.

Vivekananda was very attracted to Christianity. He created the Order of Ramakrishna based on the pattern of the Catholic priesthood. This is very alien to the East, very foreign. It is absolutely Western. Vivekananda's mind was not Eastern at all. And just as I say that Vivekananda was Western, I say that Eckhart and Saint Francis were Eastern. Basically, they belonged to the East.

Jesus himself belonged to the East. But Christianity does not belong to the East; it belongs to the West. Jesus was basically Eastern; he was antichurch, antiorganization. That was the conflict.

The Western mind thinks in terms of logic, reason, system, argument. It cannot go very deep; it will remain on the surface. It will be extensive, but never intensive.

So organized religions are a curtain to us. They will have to go in order for us to see the sky.

Yes. They cover the window. They are obstacles.

Will the Western mind have to expand as the Eastern mind has?

The Western mind can succeed as far as science is concerned, but it cannot succeed in religious consciousness. Whenever a religious mind is born, even in the West, it is Eastern. In Eckhart, in Böhme, the very quality of the mind is Eastern. And whenever a scientific mind is born in the East, it is bound to be Western. East and West are not geographical. "West" means the Aristotelian and "East" means the nonAristotelian. "West" means equilibrium and "East" means nonequilibrium; "West" means the rational and "East" means the irrational.

Tertullian was one of the most Eastern minds in the West. He said, "I believe in God because it is impossible to believe. I believe in God because it is absurd." This is the basic Eastern attitude: *because* it is absurd. No one can say this in the West. In the West they say that you should believe something only when it is rational. Otherwise it is just a belief, a superstition.

Eckhart too is an Eastern mind. He says, "If you believe in the possible, it is no belief. If you believe in the argument, it is not religion. These are parts of science. Only if you believe in the absurd does something that is beyond mind come to you." This concept is not Western. It belongs to the East.

Confucius, on the other hand, is a Western mind. Those in the West can understand Confucius, but they can never understand Lao Tzu. Lao Tzu says, "You are a fool because you are only rational. To be rational, reasonable, is not enough. The irrational must have its own corner to exist. Only if a person is both rational and irrational is he reasonable."

A totally rational person can never be reasonable. Reason has its own dark corner of irrationality. A child is born in a dark womb. A flower is born in the dark, in the underground roots. The dark must not be denied; it is the base. It is the most significant, the most life-giving thing.

The Western mind has something to contribute to the world. It is science, not religion. The Eastern mind can contribute only religion, not technology or science. Science and religion are complementary. If we can realize both their differences and their complementariness, then a better world culture can be born out of it.

If one needs science, one should go to the West. But if the West creates any religion, it can never be more than theology. In the West you give arguments to yourself to prove God. Arguments to prove God! It is inconceivable in the East. You cannot prove God. The very effort is meaningless. That which can be proven will never be God; it will be a scientific conclusion. In the East we say that the divine is the unprovable. When you are bored with your proofs, then jump into the experience itself; jump into the divine itself.

The Eastern mind can only be pseudoscientific, just as the Western mind can only be psuedoreligious. You have created a great theology in the West, not a religious tradition. In the same way, whenever wc make an attempt toward science in the East, we only create technicians not scientists, persons of know-how not innovators, creators.

So do not come to the East with a Western mind or you will only misunderstand. Then you will carry your misunderstanding as an understanding. The attitude in the East is categorically opposite. Only opposites are complementary—like male and female.

The Eastern mind is female; the Western mind is male. The Western mind is aggressive. Logic is bound to be aggressive, violent. Religion is receptive, just like a woman. God can only be received; he can never be discovered or invented. One has to become like a woman: totally receptive, just open and waiting. This is what is meant by meditation: to be open and waiting.

Ramakrishna said that the bhakti *approach is the most suitable for this age. Is that so?*

No. Ramakrishna said that *bhakti* yoga was the most suitable approach because it was the most suitable for him. That is the basic window through which he came under the sky. It is not a question of an approach being suitable or unsuitable for a particular age. We cannot think in terms of ages.

Centuries live contemporaneously. We seem to be contempories; we may not be. I may be living twenty centuries back. Nothing is absolutely past. For someone it is present. Nothing is absolutely future. For someone it is present. And nothing is absolutely present either. For someone it is past and for someone else it is yet to come. So no categorical statement can be made for the age as such.

Ramakrishna was a devotee. He came to God through prayer and love, through emotion. He realized in this way, so for him it seemed that this would be helpful to everybody. He could not understand how his way might be difficult to others. However sympathetic we may be, we always see others in the light of our own experiences. So for Ramakrishna, the way seemed to be *bhakti* yoga: the way of devotion.

If we want to think in terms of ages, we can say that this age is the most intellectual, the most scientific, the most technological —the least devotional, the least emotional. What Ramakrishna was saying was right for him might have been right for the people who were with him, but Ramakrishna never affected the larger world. He belongs basically to the village, to the nontechnological, nonscientific mind. He was a villager—uneducated, unacquainted with the greater world—so what he said should be understood according to his village language. He could not conceive of the days that have now come. He was basically part of the peasant's world where intellect was nothing and emotion was everything. He was not a man of this age. What he was saying was all right for the world in which he moved, but not for the world that exists now.

These three types have always existed: the intellectual, the active, the emotional. There will always be a balance among them, just as there is always a balance between males and females. The balance cannot be lost for long. If it is lost, it will soon be regained.

In the West you have lost the balance. Intellect has become the predominant factor. It may appeal to you that Ramakrishna says, "Devotion is the path for this age," because you have lost the balance. But Vivekananda says the opposite. Because the East has also lost the balance, he is predominantly intellectual. This is just to balance the existing extreme. It is complementary in a sense.

Ramakrishna was the emotional type and his chief disciple was the intellectual type. He was bound to be. That is the coupling: the male and the female. Ramakrishna is absolutely female: nonaggressive, receptive. Sex not only exists in biology; it exists everywhere. In every field, whenever there is polarity there is sex and the opposite becomes attracted.

Vivekananda could never be attracted to any intellectual. He could not be; he was not the polar opposite. There were intellectual giants in Bengal. He would go to visit them and would come away empty-handed. He would not be attracted. Ramakrishna was the least intellectual person possible. He was everything that Vivekananda was not, everything that he was seeking.

Vivekananda was the opposite of Ramakrishna, so what he taught in Ramakrishna's name was not in the same spirit as Ramakrishna's teaching itself. So whoever comes to Ramakrishna through Vivekananda can never come to Ramakrishna at all. Whoever understands Vivekananda's interpretation of Ramakrishna can never understand Ramakrishna himself. The interpretation comes from the polar opposite.

When people say, "Without Vivekananda we would never have known about Ramakrishna," it is right in a sense. The world-at-large would never have heard about Ramakrishna without Vivekananda. But with Vivekananda, whatever is known about Ramakrishna is basically false. It is a misinterpretation. This is because his type is quite contrary to Ramakrishna's type. Ramakrishna never argued; Vivekananda was argumentative. Ramakrishna was ignorant; Vivekananda was a man of knowledge. What Vivekananda said about Ramakrishna was said through the mirror of Vivekananda. It was never authentic. It couldn't be.

This has always been happening. It will go on happening. Buddha attracts persons who are the polar opposite to him. Mahavir and Jesus attract persons who are spiritually the other sex. These opposites then create the organization, the order. They will interpret. The very disciples will be the falsifiers. But this is what is so. It cannot be helped.

11

Right Questioning

Do not ask theoretical questions. Theories solve less and confuse more. If there were no theories, there would be less problems. It is not that theories solve questions or problems. On the contrary, questions arise *out* of theories.

And do not ask philosophical questions. Philosophical questions only seem to be questions, but they are not. That is why no answer has been possible. If a question is really a question then it is answerable, but if it is false, just a linguistic confusion, then it cannot be answered. Philosophy has gone on answering for centuries and centuries, but the questions still remain the same. However you answer a philosophical question you never answer it, because the question itself is false. It is not meant to be answered at all. The question is such that, intrinsically, no answer is possible.

And do not ask metaphysical questions. For example, if you ask who created the world, it is unanswerable. It is absurd. It is not that metaphysical questions are not real questions, but they cannot be answered. They can be solved, but they cannot be answered.

Ask questions that are personal, intimate, existential. One must be aware of what one is really asking. Is it something that really means something to you? If it is answered, will a new dimension open for you? Will something be added to your existence, will your being in any way be transformed through it? Only such questions are religious.

Religion is concerned with problems, not with questions. A question may just come out of curiosity, but a problem is intimate and personal. You are involved in it; it is you. A question is separate from you; a problem is you. So before asking anything, dig deep inside and ask something that is intimate and personal, something in which you are confused, in which you are involved. Only then can you be helped.

Are our lives predestined or not?

This is not a personal problem, it is a philosophical question.

Our lives are both predestined and they are not. Both yes and no. And both answers are true for all questions about life.

In a way, everything is predetermined. Whatever is physical in you, material, whatever is mental, is predetermined. But something in you constantly remains undetermined, unpredictable. That something is your consciousness.

If you are identified with your body and your material existence, in the same proportion you are determined by cause and effect. Then you are a machine. But if you are not identified with your material existence, with either body or mind—if you can feel yourself as something separate, different, above and transcendent to body/mind—then that transcending consciousness is not predetermined. It is spontaneous, free. Consciousness means freedom; matter means slavery. So it depends on how you define yourself. If you say, "I am only the body," then everything about you is completely determined.

A person who says that man is only the body cannot say that man is not predetermined. Ordinarily, persons who do not believe in such a thing as consciousness also do not believe in predetermination; while persons who are religious and believe in consciousness ordinarily believe in predetermination. So what I am saying may look very contradictory. But still, it is the case.

A person who has known consciousness has known freedom. So only a spiritual person can say there is no determination at all. That realization comes only when you are completely unidentified with the body. If you feel that you are just a material existence, then no freedom is possible. With matter, no freedom is possible. Matter means that which cannot be free. It must flow in the chain of cause and effect.

Once someone has achieved consciousness, enlightenment, he is completely out of the realm of cause and effect. He becomes absolutely unpredictable. You cannot say anything about him. He begins to live each moment; his existence becomes atomic.

Your existence is a riverlike chain in which every step is determined by the past. Your future is not really future; it is just a by-product of the past. It is only the past determining, shaping, formulating and conditioning your future. That is why your future is predictable.

Skinner says that man is as predictable as anything else. The only difficulty is that we have not yet devised the means to know his total past. The moment we can know his past, we can predict everything about him. Based upon the people he has worked with, Skinner is right because they are all ultimately predictable. He has experimented with hundreds of people and he has found that they are all mechanical beings, that nothing exists within them that can be called freedom.

But his study is limited. No Buddha has come to his laboratory to be experimented upon. If even one person is free, if even one person is not mechanical, not predictable, Skinner's whole theory falls. If *one* person in the whole history of mankind is free and unpredictable, then man is potentially free and unpredictable.

The whole possibility of freedom depends on whether you emphasize your body or your consciousness. If you are just an outward flow of life, then everything is determined. Or are you something inner also? Do not give any preformulated answer. Do not say, "I am the soul." If you feel there is nothing inside you, then be honest about it. This honesty will be the first step toward the inner freedom of consciousness.

If you go deeply inside, you will feel that everything is just part of the outside. Your body has come from without, your thoughts have come from without, even your self has been given to you by others. That is why you are so fearful of the opinion of others—because they are completely in control of your self. They can change their opinion of you at any moment. Your self, your body, your thoughts are given to you by others, so what is inside? You are layers and layers of outside accumulation. If you are identified with this personality of yours that comes from others, then everything is determined.

Become aware of everything that comes from the outside and become nonidentified with it. Then a moment will come when the outside falls completely. You will be in a vacuum. This vacuum is the passage between the outside and the inside, the door.

We are so afraid of the vacuum, so afraid of being empty that we cling to the outside accumulation. One has to be courageous enough to disidentify with the accumulation and to remain in the vacuum. If you are not courageous enough, you will go out and cling to something, and be filled with it. But this moment of being in the vacuum is meditation. If you are courageous enough, if you can remain in this moment, soon your whole being will automatically turn inward.

When there is nothing to be attached to from the outside, your being turns inward. Then you know for the first time that you are something that transcends everything you have been thinking yourself to be. Now you are something different from becoming; you are being. This being is free; nothing can determine it. It is absolute freedom. No chain of cause and effect is possible.

Your actions are related to past actions. *A* created a situation for *B* to become possible; *B* creates a situation in which *C* flowers. Your acts are connected to past acts and this goes back to the beginningless beginning and on to the endless end. Not only your own acts determine you, but your father's and mother's acts also have a continuity with yours. Your society, your history, all that has happened before, is somehow related to your present act. The whole history has come to flower in you.

Everything that has ever happened is connected with your act, so your act is obviously determined. It is such a minute part of the whole picture. History is such a vital living force and your individual act is such a small part of it.

Marx said, "It is not consciousness that determines the conditions of society. It is society and its conditions that determines consciousness. It is not that great men create great societies. It is great societies that create great men." And he is right in a way, because you are not the originator of your actions. The whole history has determined them. You are just carrying them out.

The whole evolutionary process has gone into the making of your biological cells. These cells in you can then become part of another person. You may think that you are the father, but you have just been a stage on which the whole biological evolution has acted and has forced you to act. The act of procreation is so forceful because it is beyond you; it is the whole evolutionary process working through you.

This is one way in which acts happen in relation to other past acts. But when a person becomes enlightened, a new phenomenon begins to happen. Acts are no longer connected with past acts. Any act, now, is connected only with his consciousness. It comes from his consciousness not from the past. That is why an enlightened person cannot be predicted.

Skinner says that we can determine what you will do if your past acts are known. He says that the old proverb, "You can lead a horse to water but you can't make him drink," is wrong. You can force him to. You can create an atmosphere so that the horse will have to drink. The horse can be forced, and you also can be forced, because your actions are created by situations, by circumstances. But even though you can bring a Buddha to the river, you cannot force him to drink. The more you force him, the more impossible it will be. No heat will make him do it. Even if a thousand suns shine on him it will not help. A Buddha has a different origin of action. It is not concerned with other acts; it is connected with consciousness.

That is why I emphasize that you act consciously. Then, every moment you act, it is not a question of a continuation of other acts. You are free. Now *you* begin to act, and no one can say how you will act.

Habits are mechanical; they repeat themselves. The more you repeat something, the more efficient you become. Efficiency means that now consciousness is no longer needed. If a person is an efficient typist it means that no effort is needed; typing can be done unconsciously. Even if he is thinking about something else the typing continues. The body is typing; the man is not needed. Efficiency means that the thing is so certain that no error is possible. With freedom, error is always possible. A machine cannot make errors. To err, one has to be conscious.

So your acts have a chain relationship with your previous acts. They are determined. Your childhood determines your youth; your youth determines your old age. Your birth determines your death; everything is determined. Buddha used to say, "Provide the cause, and the effect will be there." This is the world of cause and effect in which everything is determined.

If you act with total consciousness, an altogether different situation exists. Then everything is moment to moment. Consciousness is a flow; it is not static. It is life itself, so it changes. It is alive. It goes on expanding; it goes on becoming new, fresh, young. Then, your acts will be spontaneous.

I am reminded of a Zen story. A Zen master asked his disciple a particular question. The question was answered exactly as it should be answered. The next day the master asked exactly the same question. The disciple said, "But I answered this question yesterday."

The master said, "Now I am asking you again." The disciple repeated the same answer. The master said, "You do not know!"

The disciple said, "But yesterday I answered in the same way and you nodded your head. So I interpreted that the answer was right. Why have you changed your mind now?"

The master said, "Anything that can be repeated is not coming from you. The answer has come from your memory, not from your consciousness. If you had really known, the answer would be different because so much has changed. I am not the same man who asked you this question yesterday. The whole situation is different. You also are different, but the answer is the same. I had to ask the question again just to see if you would repeat the answer. Nothing can be repeated."

The more alive you are, the less repetitive. Only a dead man can be consistent. Living is inconsistency; life is freedom. Freedom cannot be consistent. Consistent with what? You can be consistent only with the past.

An enlightened person is consistent only in his consciousness; he is never consistent with his past. He is totally in the act. Nothing is left behind; nothing is left out. The next moment the act is finished and his consciousness is fresh again. Consciousness will be there whenever any situation arises, but each act will be made in complete freedom, as if it is the first time that this man has been in this particular situation.

That is why I answered both yes and no to your question. It depends on you—on whether you are consciousness, or whether you are an accumulation, a bodily existence.

Religion gives freedom because religion gives consciousness. The more science knows about matter, the more the world will be enslaved. The whole phenomenon of matter is of cause and effect. If you know that given "this," "that" happens, then everything can be determined.

Before this century ends, we will see the whole course of humanity being determined in many ways. The greatest calamity that is possible is not nuclear warfare. It can only destroy. The real calamity will come from the psychological sciences. They will learn how a human being can be completely controlled. Because we are not conscious, we can be made to behave in predetermined ways.

As we are, everything about us is determined. Someone is Hindu; someone else is Mohammedan. This is predetermination, not freedom. Parents have decided; society is deciding. Someone is a doctor and someone else is an engineer. Now his behavior is determined.

We are already being controlled constantly, and our methods are still very primitive. Newer techniques will be able to determine our behavior to such an extent that no one will be able to say that there is a soul. If your every response is determined, then what is the meaning of the soul?

Your responses can be determined through body chemistry. If alcohol is given to you, you behave differently. Your body chemistry is different so you behave differently. At one time, the ultimate tantra technique was to take intoxicants and remain conscious. If a person remained conscious when everything indicated that he should be unconscious, only then would tantra say the man was enlightened, otherwise not.

If body chemistry can change your consciousness, then what is the meaning of consciousness? If an injection can make you unconscious, then what is the meaning? Then the chemical drug in the injection is more powerful than your own consciousness. Tantra says it is possible to transcend every intoxicant and remain conscious. The stimulus has been given, but the response is not there.

Sex is a chemical phenomenon. A particular quantity of a particular hormone creates sexual desire. You become the desire. You may repent when your body chemistry has returned to its normal level, but the repentance is meaningless. When the hormones are there again, you will act in the same way. So tantra has also experimented with sex. If you feel no sexual desire in a situation that is totally sexual, then you are free. Your body chemistry has been left far behind. The body is there, but you are not in the body.

Anger is also just chemistry. Biochemists will soon be able to make you anger-proof, or sex-proof. But you will not be a Buddha.

Buddha was not incapable of anger. He was capable of it, but the effect of feeling anger was not there.

If your body chemistry is controlled, you will be incapable of being angry. The chemical condition that makes you feel angry is not there, so the effect of anger is not there. Or if your sex hormones are eliminated from your body, you will not be sexual. But the real thing is not whether you are sexual or not, or angry or not. The real thing is how to be aware in a situation that requires your unawareness, how to be conscious in a situation that happens only in unconsciousness.

Whenever such a situation is there, meditate on it. You have been given a great opportunity. If you feel jealous, meditate on it. This is the right moment. Your body chemistry is working within you. It will make you unconscious; it will make you behave as if you are mad. Now, be conscious. Let there be jealousy, do not suppress it, but be conscious; be a witness to it.

If there is anger, be a witness to it; if there is sex, be a witness to it. Let whatever is happening inside you happen, and begin to meditate on the whole situation. By and by, the more your awareness deepens, the less possibility there is of your behavior being determined for you. You become free. *Moksha*, freedom, doesn't mean anything else. It only means a consciousness that is so free that now nothing can determine it.

What is divine love? How does an enlightened person experience love?

First let us look at the question itself. You must have been waiting to ask it. It couldn't have come to you just now; you must have decided on it in advance. It was waiting to be asked; it was forcing you to ask it. Your memory has determined the asking, not your consciousness. If you were conscious right now, if you were in the moment, this question would not have come. If you had been listening to what I have been saying, this question would be impossible.

If the question has been present in you, it is impossible for you to have heard anything I have been saying. A question that is constantly present in the mind creates a tension and because of the tension you cannot be here. That is why your consciousness cannot act with freedom. If you understand this, then we can take up your question.

The question itself is good, but the mind that has been thinking about it is ill. Awareness must be there moment to moment, not only in acts but in questions, in every gesture. If I raise my finger, it may be just a habit. Then I am not the master of my body. But if it is a spontaneous expression of something that is present in my consciousness right now, it is altogether different.

A Christian preacher's every gesture is predetermined. He has been taught it. Once I was at a Christian theological college. After five years at this school, one becomes a doctor of divinity. Absurd! A doctor of divinity is sheer idiocy! They were being trained in everything: how to stand on the pulpit, how to begin the service, how to sing the hymn, how to look at the audience, where to stop and where to leave a gap or interval. Everything! This foolish preparation must not happen. It is a great misfortune.

So be in the moment. Do not decide anything beforehand. Be aware that the question is present in you, that it is knocking at the door of the mind continuously. You were not hearing me at all—just because of this question! And when I begin talking about your question, your mind will create another question. Again you will miss. What I am saying is not personal to you. It is true for everyone.

Now the question.

Whenever love exists it is divine, so to say "divine love" is meaningless. Love is always divine. But the mind is cunning. It says: "We know what love is. It is only that we do not know what *divine* love is." But we do not even know love. It is one of the most unknown things. There is too much talk about it; it is never lived. This is a trick of the mind. We talk about that which we cannot live.

Literature, music, poetry, dance—everything revolves around love. If love were really there, we would not talk about it so much. Our excessive talk about love shows that love is nonexistent. Speaking about things which are not is a substitute. By talking, by language, by symbols, by art, we create an illusion that the thing is there. One who has never known love may write a better poem about it than one who has known love, because the vacuum is much deeper. It has to be filled. Something has to be substituted in place of love.

It is better to understand what love is first, because when you ask about divine love it is understood that love is known. But love is not known. What is known as love is something else. The false must be known before steps can be taken toward the real, the true.

What is known as love is just infatuation. You begin to love someone. If that someone becomes yours totally, love will die soon; but if there are barriers, if you cannot have the person you love, the love will become intense. The more barriers, the more intensely love will be felt. If the beloved or the lover is impossible to get, the love becomes eternal; but if you can win your lover easily, then the love dies easily.

When you try to get something and you cannot get it, you become intense about getting it. The more hindrances there are, the more your ego feels it is necessary to do something. It becomes an ego problem. The more you are denied, the more tense you become—and the more infatuated. This tension you call love. That is why, once the honeymoon is over, the love is old. Even before that. What you knew as love was not love. It was just ego infatuation, ego tension: a struggle, a conflict.

Ancient human societies were very cunning. They devised methods to make love last. If a man cannot see his wife for a long time, infatuation will be created; tension will be created. Then a man can remain with one wife his whole life.

But in the West now, marriage cannot exist anymore. It is not that the Western mind is more sexual. It is that infatuation is not allowed to accumulate. Sex is so easily available that marriage cannot exist. Love too cannot exist with this kind of freedom. If a society is completely free sexually, then only sex can exist.

Boredom is the other side of infatuation. If you love someone and do not win the loved one, the infatuation goes deep; but if you win him or her, you begin to feel bored, fed up, There are many dualities: infatuation/boredom, love/hate, attraction/repulsion. With infatuation you feel attraction, love, and with boredom you feel repulsion, hate.

No attraction can really be love because repulsion is bound to come. It is in the very nature of things that the other side will come. If you do not want the opposite to come, you must create barriers so that infatuation never ends; you must create daily tensions. Then infatuation continues. This is the reason for the whole ancient system of creating barriers to love.

But soon it will no longer be possible. Then marriage will die, and love will also die. It will go deep in the background. Only sex will remain. But sex cannot stand by itself; it becomes too mechanical. Neitzsche declared that God is dead. The real thing that is going to be dead in this century is sex. I don't mean that people will be nonsexual. They will be sexual, but the excessive emphasis on sex will go. Sex will become an ordinary act like anything else—like urinating or eating or anything. It will not be meaningful. It has become meaningful only because of the barriers that have been created around it.

What you have been calling love is not love. It is just delayed sex. Then what is love? Love is not related to sex at all. Sex may come into it or it may not, but it is not really related to sex at all. It is a different thing altogether.

To me, love is a by-product of a meditative mind. It is not related to sex; it is related to *dhyana*, meditation. The more silent you become, the more at ease with yourself you will be, the more fulfilled you will feel, and the more a new expression of your being will be there. You will begin to love. Not anyone in particular. It may happen with someone in particular, but that is another thing. You begin to *love*. This loving becomes your way of existing. It can never turn into repulsion because it is not an attraction.

You must understand the distinction clearly. Ordinarily when you fall in love with someone, the real feeling is how to get love from him. It is not that love is going from you to him. Rather, it is an expectation that love will come to you *from* him. That is why love becomes possessive. You possess someone so that you can get something out of him. But the love I am talking about is neither possessive nor does it have any expectations. It is just how you behave. You have become so silent, so loving, that your silence goes to others now.

When you are angry, your anger goes to others. When you hate, your hate goes to others. When you are in love, you feel that your love is going out to others, but you are not dependable. One moment there is love, and the next moment there will be hate. Hate is not opposite to love; it is part and parcel of it, a continuity.

If you have loved someone, then you will hate him. You may not be courageous enough to admit it, but you will hate him. Lovers are always in conflict when they are together. When they are not together they may sing songs of love to each other, but when they are together they are always fighting. They cannot live alone, and they cannot live together. When the other is not there, infatuation is created; the two again feel love for one another. But when the other is present, infatuation goes and hatred is felt again.

The love I am talking about means that you have become so silent that now there is neither anger nor attraction nor repulsion. Really, now there is no love and no hate. You are not other-oriented at all. The other has disappeared; you are alone with yourself. In this feeling of aloneness, love comes to you like a fragrance.

To ask for love from the other is always ugly. To depend on the other, to ask for something from the other, always creates bondage, suffering, conflict. A person should be sufficient unto himself. What I mean by meditation is a state of being where a person is sufficient unto himself. You have become a circle, alone. The mandala is complete.

You are trying to make the mandala complete with others: man with woman, woman with man. At certain moments the lines meet, but almost before they have met the separation begins. Only if you become a perfect circle—whole, sufficient unto yourself—does love begin to flower in you. Then whatever comes near you, you love. It is not an act at all; it is not something that you do. Your very being, your very presence, is love. Love flows through you.

If you ask a person who has reached this state, "Do you love me?" it will be difficult for him to answer. He cannot say, "I love you," because it is not an act on his part; it is not a doing. And he cannot say, "I do not love you," because he loves. Really, he *is* love.

This love comes only with the freedom I have been talking about. Freedom is the feeling you have, and love is the feeling others have about you. When meditation happens inside, you feel completely free. This freedom is an inner feeling; it cannot be felt by others.

Sometimes your behavior may create difficulties for others, because they cannot conceive of what has happened in you. In a way you will be a trouble to them, an inconvenience, because you cannot be predicted. Now nothing will be known about you. What will you do next? What will you say? No one can know. Everyone around you feels a certain inconvenience. They can never be at ease with you because now you are likely to do anything; you are not dead.

They cannot feel your freedom because they have not known anything like it. They have not even looked for it; they have not sought it. They are so much in bondage that they cannot even conceive of what freedom is. They have been in cages, they have not known the open sky, so even if you talk to them about the open sky it cannot be communicated to them. But they can feel your love, because they have been asking for love. Even in their cages, in their bondage, they have been searching for love. They have created the whole bondage—bondage with persons, with things—only because of their search for love.

So whenever a person happens to be free, his love is felt. But you will feel that love as compassion not as love, because there will be no excitement in it. It will be very diffused—with no heat, with no warmth even. There is no excitement in it. It is there, that's all. Excitement comes and goes, it cannot be constant, so if there is excitement in Buddha's love then Buddha will have to move into hate again. So excitement will not be there. Peaks will not be there, and valleys will not be there. The love is just there. You will feel it as *karuna*, compassion.

Freedom cannot be felt from the outside; only love can be felt. And that too only as compassion. This has been one of the most difficult phenomena of human history. The freedom of an enlightened one creates inconvenience, and their love is compassion. That is why society is always divided about these people.

There are people who have felt only the inconvenience that a Christ creates. These are the people who are well-established. They do not need compassion. They think that they have love, health, wealth, respect, everything. Christ happens and the "haves" will be against him because he will be creating an inconvenience for them, while the "have-nots" will be for him because they will feel his compassion. They are in need of love. No one has loved them, but this man loves them. They will not feel the inconvenience of a Christ because they have nothing to fear, nothing to lose.

When a Christ dies everyone will feel his compassion, because now there is no inconvenience. Even the well-established will feel at ease; they will worship him. But when he is living, he is a rebel. And he is a rebel because he is free.

He is not a rebel because something is wrong with society. Such rebelliousness is only political. If the society changes, the very one who was rebellious will become orthodox. This happened in 1917. The very revolutionaries became one of the most antirevolutionary cliques in the world. The moment men like Stalin or Mao are in power they become the most antirevolutionary leaders possible because they are not really rebellious. They are only rebelling against a particular situation. Once that situation is overthrown, they become the same as those they fought to overthrow.

But a Christ is always rebellious. No situation will extinguish his rebellion, because his rebellion is not *against* anyone. It is because his consciousness is free. Anywhere he feels a barrier, he will feel rebellious. The rebellion is his spirit. So if Jesus comes today, Christians will not be at ease with him. They are part of the establishment now; they have become settled. If Jesus comes into the marketplace again he will destroy everything they have. The Vatican, the Church, is not possible with Jesus. Only without Jesus is it possible.

Every teacher who has achieved enlightenment is rebellious, but the tradition that is concerned with him is never rebellious. It is never concerned with his rebellion, with his freedom, but only with his compassion, his love. But then it becomes impotent. Love cannot exist without freedom, without rebellion.

You cannot be as loving as Buddha unless you are as free as he. A Buddhist monk is just *trying* to be compassionate. The compassion is impotent because the freedom is not there. Freedom is the source. Mahavir is compassionate, but a Jain monk is not compassionate at all. He is just *acting* nonviolently and compassionately; he is not really compassionate. He is cunning. Even in his compassion, and his exhibition of it, he is cunning. There is no compassion, because the freedom is not there.

Whenever freedom happens in human consciousness, freedom is felt from inside and love is felt from outside. This love, this compassion, is an absence of both love and hate. The complete dualism is absent; there is neither attraction nor repulsion.

So with a person who is free and loving, it depends on you whether you can take his love or not. It is not up to me how much love I can give you; it depends on how much love you can take. Ordinarily love depends on the person who is giving. He may give love; he may not. But the love I am talking about is not dependent on the giver. He is completely open and giving every moment. Even when no one is present, the love is flowing.

It is just like a flower in the desert. No one may know that it has flowered and is giving out its perfume, but it will give it. It is not being given to anyone; it is just being given. The flower has bloomed, so the fragrance is there. Whether someone passes or not is irrelevant. If someone passes and is sensitive he may receive it. But if he is completely dead, insensitive, he may not even be aware that there is a flower there.

When love is there, it is up to you whether you can receive it or not. Only when love is *not* there can the other give it to you or withhold it from you. With love, with compassion, there is no division between divine and nondivine. Love *is* divine. God is love.

12

Balancing the Rational and the Irrational

What factors do you attribute the Western youth revolt to, and why are so many young people from the West now becoming interested in Eastern religion and philosophy?

Mind is a very contradictory thing. It works in polar opposites. But our logical way of thinking always chooses one part and denies the other. So logic proceeds in a noncontradictory way, and mind works in a contradictory way. Mind works in opposites, and logic works linearly.

For example, the mind has two possibilities: to be angry or to be silent. If you can be angry it does not mean that at the other extreme you cannot also be nonangry. If you can be disturbed it does not mean that you cannot be silent. The mind goes on working in both ways. If you can be loving you can be full of hatred also. One doesn't deny the other.

But if you are loving you begin to think you are incapable of hate. Then hate goes on accumulating inside and when you reach the peak of your loving, everything shatters. You sink into hate. And not only does the rational mind work like that; society does also.

The West has come to a peak of rational thinking. Now the irrational part of the mind will take revenge. The irrational has been denied expression and in the last fifty years it has been taking its revenge in so many ways: through art, poetry, drama, literature, philosophy. And now, even through living. So the revolt of the young is really a revolt of the irrational part of the mind against too much rationality.

The East can be helpful to those in the West because the East has lived with the other part of the mind: the irrational. It has also reached a peak: a peak of irrationality. Now young people in the East are more interested in communism than in religion, more interested in rational thinking than in irrational living. As I see it, the whole pendulum will turn now. The East will become like the West, and the West will become like the East.

Whenever one part of the mind reaches a peak, you move to the opposite. That is what always happens in history. So in the West now, meditation will be more meaningful. Poetry will gain a new hold and science will decline. Modern-day Western youth will be antitechnological, antiscientific. This is a natural process, an automatic balancing of the extreme.

We have not yet been able to develop a personality that combines both polarities, that is neither Eastern nor Western. We have always chosen only one part of the mind and the opposite part remains hungry, starved. Then there is bound to be rebellion. Everything that we have worked to develop will be shattered, and the mind will move to the other polarity. This has happened throughout history; this has been the dialectic.

For the West now, meditation will be more meaningful than thinking because meditation means no-thinking. Zen will be more appealing, Buddhism will be more appealing, yoga will be more appealing. These are all irrational attitudes toward life. They do not emphasize conceptualizations, theories, theologies. They emphasize a zest to move deep into existence, not into thinking. As I see it, the more grip technology has on the mind, the more likely it is that the other pole will be coming.

The revolt of young people in the West is very meaningful, very significant. It is a historical point of change, a whole change of consciousness. Now the West cannot continue as it has been. A point of deep crisis has come. The West will have to move in another direction now.

The whole society in the West is affluent now. Individuals have been affluent before, but never the whole society. When a society becomes affluent, riches lose their meaning. They are meaningful only in a poor society. But even in a poor society, when someone becomes really affluent he is bored. The more sensitive a person is, the sooner he becomes bored. A Buddha is just bored. He leaves everything.

The whole attitude of modern youth is one of boredom with an empty affluence. The youth are leaving the society, and they will go on leaving it unless the whole society becomes poor. Then they will not be able to leave. This leaving, this renunciation, can exist only in an affluent society. If it is taken to an extreme, the society will decline. Then technology will not progress, and if this continues the West will become like the East is today.

In the East they are turning to the other extreme. They will create a society just like that of the West. The East is turning to the West and the West is turning to the East, but the disease remains the same. As I see it, the disease is the imbalance, the acceptance of one thing and the denial of the other.

We have never allowed the human mind to flower in its totality. We have always chosen one part against the other, at the cost of the other. This has been the misery. So I am neither for the Eastern way nor the Western way. I am against both, because they are partial attitudes. One should choose neither the East nor the West; they have both failed. The East has failed by choosing religion and the West is failing by choosing science. Unless both are chosen there is no way out of this vicious circle.

We can change from one extreme to the other. If you talk about Buddhism in Japan, no young person is ready to listen. They are interested in technology, and you are interested in Zen Buddhism. In India, the new generation is not interested in religion in the least. They are interested in economics, in politics, in technology, engineering, science—in everything except religion. Youth in the West is interested in religion while youth in the East is interested in science. This is just changing the burden from one extreme to another. The same fallacy will still exist.

I am interested in the total mind, in a mind that is neither Eastern nor Western, that is just human—a global mind. It is easy to live with one part of the mind, but if you want to live with both parts you will have to live a very inconsistent life. Inconsistent superficially of course. On a deeper layer you will have a consistency, a spiritual harmony.

Man remains spiritually poor unless the opposite polarity is also a part of him. Then he becomes rich. If you are simply an artist and have no scientific mind, your art is bound to be poor. Richness comes only when the opposite is there. If there are only males in the room, the room lacks something. The moment females enter, the room becomes spiritually rich. Now, the polar opposites are both there. The whole becomes greater.

The mind must not be fixed. A mathematician will be richer if he can move into the world of arts. If his mind has the freedom to move away from its main fixations and then back to them again, he will be a richer mathematician. Through the opposite, a cross-breeding happens. You begin to look at things in a different way. Your total perspective will be richer.

A person should have a religious mind along with scientific training, a scientific mind along with religious discipline. I see no inherent impossibility in it. On the contrary, I think the mind will become more alive if it can move from one to the other. To me, meditation means an ability to move deeply in all directions, a freedom from fixations.

For example, if I become too logical then I become incapable of understanding poetry. Logic becomes a fixation. Then when I listen to poetry, my fixation is there. The poetry looks absurd. Not because it is, but because I have a fixation with logic. From the viewpoint of logic, poetry *is* absurd. On the other hand, if I become fixated on poetry then I begin to think of logic as just a utilitarian thing, with no depth in it. I become closed to it.

This denial of one part by the other has been happening throughout history. Every period, every nation, every part of the world, every culture has always chosen one part and created a personality around it. The personality was poor, lacking much. Neither the East has been rich spiritually nor the West. They cannot be. Richness comes through opposites, through the inner dialectic. To me, neither the East is worth choosing nor the West. A different quality of mind must be chosen. By that quality I mean that one is at rest with oneself, without choosing.

A tree grows. We can cut down all the branches except one and allow the tree to grow only in one direction. It will be a very poor tree, very ugly, and ultimately it is bound to be in deep difficulty because a single branch cannot grow by itself; it can grow only in a family of branches. A moment is bound to come when the branch will feel it has reached a cul-de-sac. Now it cannot grow anymore. For a tree to really grow it must be allowed to grow in all directions. Only then will the tree be rich, strong.

The human spirit must grow like a tree: in all directions. The concept that we cannot grow in opposite directions must be dropped. Really, we can grow *only* if we grow in opposite directions. Up until now we have been saying that one must specialize, one must grow in one specific direction only. Then something ugly happens. One grows in a specific direction, and he lacks everything. He becomes a branch not a tree. And even this branch is bound to be poor.

Not only have we been cutting the branches of the mind, but we have been cutting the roots. We allow only one root and only one branch, so a very starved human being has developed all over the world: in the East, in the West, everywhere. Then those in the East are attracted to the West and those in the West to the East, because one is attracted to what one lacks.

Because of the needs of the body, the East has begun to be attracted to the West; and because of the needs of the spirit, the West has begun to be attracted to the East. But even if we change positions, change attitudes, the disease remains the same. It is not a question of changing positions; it is a question of changing the whole perspective.

We have never accepted the whole human being. Somewhere, sex is not accepted. Somewhere else, the world is not accepted. Somewhere else, emotion is not accepted. We have never been strong enough to accept everything that is human, without condemnation, and to allow human beings to grow in every direction. The more you grow in opposite directions, the greater will be the growth, the richness, the inner affluence. Our total perspective must change. We must move from the past to the future—not from East to West, not from one present to another present.

The problem is so arduous because our fragmentation has gone so deep. I cannot accept my anger, I cannot accept my sex, I cannot accept my body, I cannot accept my totality. Something has to be denied and thrown away. "This" is evil, "this" is bad, "this" is sin. I have to go on cutting branches. Soon I am not a tree at all, not an alive thing. And the fear is always there that the branches I have denied can come up again, can grow again. I become fearful about everything. Disease sets in: a sadness, a death.

We go on living partial lives that are nearer to death than to life. One must accept the total human potentiality, bringing everything within oneself to a peak without feeling any inconsistency, any contradiction. If you cannot be authentically angry, you cannot be loving. But this has not been the attitude up to now. We have been thinking that a person is more loving if he is incapable of anger.

But supposing the tree is growing next to a wall. Its branches cannot grow because the wall is there. The wall may be society, its existing conditions. How can the tree grow when there is a wall next to it?

There are many walls. But those walls have been created by the trees, not by anyone else. The trees have been supporting the walls. It is through their cooperation that the walls exist. The moment the trees are no longer ready to support the walls, they will drop, shatter.

The walls that exist around us are our creation. Because of the attitudes of the human mind, we have created these walls. For example, you teach your child not to be angry by telling him that if he becomes angry he will not be a loving child. Then you create walls around him that tell him he must suppress his anger, without realizing that if he suppresses his anger his capacity to love will be destroyed simultaneously. Anger and love are not incompatible things. They are two branches of the same thing. If you cut one, the other becomes poor, because the same sap runs through every branch.

If you really want to train your child for a better life, you will teach him to be angry authentically. You will not say, "Do not be angry." You will say, "When you feel angry, be authentically angry, totally angry. Do not feel guilty about the anger." Rather then telling him not to be angry, train him to be rightly angry. When the right moment is there he should be authentically angry, and he should not be angry at the wrong moment. The same is true for love. When the right moment is there, he should be authentically loving; and if it is the wrong moment for him, he should not be loving.

It is not a question of choosing between anger and love. The question is between right and wrong, authentic and inauthentic. Anger must be expressed. A child, when he is really angry, is beautiful—a sudden flush of energy and life. If you kill the anger, you are killing the life. He will become impotent. For his whole life he will not be able to be alive; he will move like a dead corpse.

We go on creating concepts that create walls. We develop attitudes and ideologies that create walls. These walls are not imposed on us; they are our creations. The moment we become aware, the walls disappear. They exist because of us.

But suppose the tree (the person) is basically handicapped? Then he cannot change. Not because he doesn't want to, but because he can't.

The handicapped are not problems. When the whole society is alive, we can treat them. We can analyze them, help them. They have to be helped; they cannot do anything by themselves. But the society plays a part even in their helplessness.

For example, the son of a prostitute is handicapped because of our moral concepts. He feels a deep guilt for something that he is not at all responsible for. How can he help it that his mother was a prostitute? What can he do about it? But the society goes on behaving differently toward the boy. Until we have a different attitude toward sex, his guilt about being the son of a prostitute will continue.

Because we have made marriage sacred, prostitution is bound to be considered a sin. But prostitution exists because of marriage. It is part of the whole system of marriage.

As the human mind is, a permanent relationship is unnatural. One will continue to live with the same person indefinitely only if the law requires it. It must not be the law. It must not be forced on me that if I love someone today I must also love this same person tomorrow. It is not a requirement of nature. There is no intrinsic necessity that tomorrow the love will be there. It may be; it may not be. And the more you force it to be there, the more impossible it becomes. Then prostitution enters from the back door. Unless we have a society that allows free relationships, we cannot end prostitution.

If a relationship continues, you feel good about it; your ego feels good. To fulfill your ego—that you are a faithful husband or a satisfying wife—the prostitute has to be condemned. Then the son of the prostitute has to be condemned and it becomes a disease. A sickness is created in him.

But these are exceptional cases. If someone is medically or

psychologically ill we have to help him, treat him. But the whole society is not like that. Ninety-nine percent is our creation; one percent is the exception. The one percent is not the problem at all. If the other ninety-nine percent of society changes, even the one percent will be affected by it.

We cannot decide yet to what extent your physiology is determined by your mind. The more we know, the more uncertain we become. Many diseases in the body may be there just because of your mind. Unless one's mind is free, he cannot know for sure that the disease is originating in the body.

So many diseases are just a human phenomenon. They do not occur in animals. Animals are more healthy. Less diseased, less ugly. There is no reason why man cannot be more alive, more beautiful, more healthy. The training that we have gone through for ten thousand years, this long training of the mind, may be the root cause of it. But when you yourself are part of the same pattern, you cannot even conceive of this.

Many physical diseases exist because of a crippled mind. And we are crippling everybody's mind! The first seven years of a child's life are the most significant. If you cripple the mind, after that it becomes more difficult to change it. But we go on crippling, and with a good conscience. The more deeply psychology penetrates into the roots of the mind, the more parents seem to be criminals, but unknowingly; the more the teachers and the educational system seem to be criminals, but unknowingly. They also suffered from the older generation. They are only passing on the disease.

But now a new possibility has opened up. For the first time, particularly in the West, man is free from his day-to-day needs. Now we can experiment with new possibilities for the mind. It was impossible to do this in the past, because bodily needs were such a heavy burden, so unfulfilled. But now the possibility is there. We live on the threshold of a deep revolution, a revolution such as human history has never encountered. A revolution in consciousness is possible now. With more facilities to know and understand, we can change. Much time will be needed, but the possibility is open to us. If we dare, if we have courage, it can become an actuality.

The whole humanity is at stake. Either we will go back to the past or to a new future. It is not a question of a third world war, not a question of communism or capitalism. These problems are out of date now. A new crisis is nearby. Either we will have to decide that we want to have a new consciousness, and work for it, or we will have to fall back, to regress to the old patterns.

To regress is also possible. Whenever a crisis is there, regression is the tendency of the mind. Whenever you face something that you *cannot* face, you regress. For example, if this house is suddenly on fire, you will begin to behave like children. When the house is on fire you need more maturity, more understanding, you need to behave in a more aware way, but instead you regress to about the age of five and begin to run around in such a way that you create more danger for yourself.

The sad possibility is that if we try to create a new human being we will face a situation that is altogether new to us and we may regress. There are even prophets who preach regression. They want the past to come back: "A golden age existed in the past. Go back!" But to me, that is suicidal. We must go into the future, however hazardous and difficult it may be.

Life must move to the future. We must find a new mode of existence. I am hopeful that this can happen. And the West has to be the ground of its happening, because the East is nothing but the West of three hundred years ago. Problems of sustenance and survival weigh heavily upon the East, but the West is free of all this.

When young people from the West come to me, I am always aware that they can either progress or regress. And in a way they have been regressing, behaving like children, like primitives. That is not good. Their revolt is good, but they must behave like a new kind of man and not like primitives. They must create within themselves the possibilities for a new consciousness.

Instead, they are just drugging themselves. The primitive mind has always been enchanted with drugs, hypnotized by them. If those who are dropping out of society in the West begin to behave like primitives, it is not a rebellion but a reaction and a regression. They must behave like a new humanity. They must proceed toward a new consciousness that is total, global and accepting of all the inconsistent potentialities in a human being.

The difference between animals and man is that animals have fixed potentialities while man has infinite possibilities. But they are only possibilities. Man can grow, but this growth must be helped. We must open up centers throughout the world where this can happen.

The mind must be trained in a logical, rational way, but it must be simultaneously trained in irrational, nonrational meditation. The reason must be trained, and at the same time the emotions. Reason must not be trained at the cost of the emotions. Doubt must be there, but faith also.

It is easy to be faithful without any doubt, and it is easy to be doubtful without any faith. But these simple formulas will not do now. Now we must create a healthy doubt, a persistent doubt, a skeptical mind that exists simultaneously with a trusting mind. And the inner being must be capable of moving from one to the other: from doubt to faith, and back again. With objective research, one must be doubtful, skeptical, cautious. But there is another dimension adjacent to this where trust gives the clues not doubt. Both are needed.

The problem is how to create the contrary polarities simultaneously. This is what I am interested in. I will go on creating doubt and will go on creating faith. I do not see any inherent inconsistency in it, because for me it is the movement that is important, the movement from one pole to another.

The more we are fixed on one pole, the more difficult it becomes. For example, in the West you have cultivated activity. But you cannot sleep well. When you go to sleep and the mind needs to move from activity to inactivity, it cannot. You go on turning in your bed; the mind goes on being active. In order to sleep, you have to take a tranquilizer. But a forced sleep cannot give you much rest; it is just superficial. Deep down, the turmoil goes on. The sleep becomes a nightmare.

The opposite has happened in the East. The East can sleep well, but cannot be active. Even in the morning the Eastern mind feels lethargic, sleepy. For centuries they have been sleeping well and doing nothing else, while you have done much, but you have created unease, a dis/ease. And because of this dis/ease, everything you have done is useless. You cannot even sleep!

That is why my emphasis is to train the mind for activity, for inactivity and, most significant of all, for movement—so that you can move between the two. The mind *can* be trained to move from one to the other. From any activity, in a single moment I can move to inactivity. I can talk with you for hours and in a single moment I can move to a deep, inner silence with no talking going on. And unless this possibility is created in you, your growth will be stunted.

The future has to allow there to be a deep harmony between inner polarities. Unless this movement between opposites is created, human inquiry is finished. You cannot move ahead. The East is exhausted and the West is exhausted. You can change the perspective of the two but then, within two centuries, the same problem will again come up. If you just exchange one attitude for the other, you begin to move in a circle.

But how can one know what are the right goals to aspire to in life if everything is to be accepted?

The very search for goals is part of the rational process. The future exists because of reason. That is why for animals there is no future and no goal. They live, but there is no goal. Reason creates ideals; it creates goals; it creates the future. The real problem is not what is the right goal. The real question is whether to have goals or not.

The new generation is asking whether to have goals or not. The moment you have a goal, you begin to turn away from life. You begin to mold life according to your goals. The present becomes less meaningful. It has to be molded, adjusted to the future.

A goal-oriented mind is reason, and a life-oriented mind is irrationality. So it is not a question of how to have the right goals. The question is how to make it so that reason is not the sole phenomenon of the mind.

Reason has to have goals; it cannot exist without them. But this must not become dictatorial; it must not be the only branch growing. Reason must exist, it is a necessity, but there is an empty part of the human mind that cannot have goals, that can exist just like animals, like children. It can exist only here and now. This empty part, this irrational part, experiences the deeper realms of life, of love, of art. It has no need to go into the future, so it can go deep into the here and now. Reason must be developed, but this part must be developed simultaneously.

There have been scientists with very deeply religious personalities. This can happen in two ways. Either it can be a deep harmony, or it can be just closing one aperture and opening another, without any harmony. I can be a scientist and then I can leave my scientific world and go to church to pray. Then the scientist is not praying. It is not a harmony really; it is a deep bifurcation. There is no inner dialogue between the scientist and the worshiper. The scientist has not come to church at all.

When this man goes back to his lab, the worshiper is not there. There is a deep division between the two; they do not overlap. In such a person you will find a dichotomy not a harmony. He will say things that he himself feels guilty to have said. He will make statements as a scientist that go against his mind as a worshiper.

So many scientists have led schizophrenic lives. A part of them is one thing, and another part is something else. This is not what I mean by harmony. By harmony I mean you are capable of moving from one to the other without ever being closed to either. Then the scientist goes to pray, and the religious man goes to the lab. There is no division, no gap.

Otherwise, you will become two persons. Ordinarily we are many people; we have multi-personalities. We become identified with one, and then we change gears and become something else. This gear changing is not a harmony. It creates a very deep tension in your being. You cannot be at ease with so many identities. An undivided consciousness, capable of moving to the polar opposite, is possible only when we have a concept of the human being as intrinsically one—when there is no denial of opposites.

Doubt is part of a scientist's work. Faith is also a part. They are two aspects that look at different dimensions of the same thing. So a scientist can pray in his lab; there is nothing wrong in it. Doubt is part of his work, an instrument of his work, and so is faith. There is no inherent dichotomy. When one can move easily, smoothly, from one to the other, even the movement is not felt. You move, but the movement is not felt. Movement is only felt when there is some obstable. When there is a deep harmony, no movement is felt.

One thing more: when I say "East" and "West" I do not mean that in the West there have been no Eastern minds and in the East there have been no Western minds. I am talking about the main current. Sometime we should write a history of the world in which the world is not divided geographically but psychologically.

In it, the East will have many faces from the West and the West will have many faces from the East.

So I do not mean that both trends do not exist in the West. I mean that the main current in the West has been toward rational growth, even in religion. That is why the Church became so dominant.

Jesus was an irrational man, but Saint Paul had a very scientific mind, a very rational mind. Christianity belongs to Saint Paul, not to Jesus. With such an anarchic man there is no possibility of such a big organization. It is impossible. Jesus was Eastern—but Saint Paul was not.

There has been a conflict between science and the Church. Both are rational. Both tried to rationalize religious phenomena. The Church was bound to be defeated, because religious phenomena themselves are irrational. Reason fails as far as religion is concerned. That is why the Church had to be defeated, and science was victorious.

In the East there has been no fight between science and religion because religion has never claimed anything within the realm of reason. The two do not belong to the same category, so there is no fight between them.

How does religion become rational?

This happens not because of the religion itself. But whenever religion has to be systematized, the phenomena happens. A Buddha or a Jesus is not after any ideal. They live spontaneous lives; they grow in their own way. They grow like wild trees, but then the wild trees become ideals for their followers. The followers begin to have patterns, preferences, truths, condemnations.

Religion has two parts. One, a deeply religious personality who is spontaneous; and two, the followers who create the creed, the dogma, the discipline according to the ideal. Then an ideal exists for Buddhists—"One must be like Buddha"—and suppressions are created. You have to destroy yourself in many ways, because only then can you become the ideal. You have to become an imitation.

To me, this is criminal. A religious personality is beautiful, but a religious creed is just a rational thing. It is just reason encountering a nonrational phenomenon.

Didn't Buddha have a rational mind?

He was very rational, but he had very irrational gaps. He was at ease with the irrational also. The concept we have of Buddha is not really of Buddha, but of the traditions that followed. Buddha was an altogether different thing.

But because we cannot do otherwise, we have to go through Buddhists to reach Buddha. They have created a long tradition of two thousand years, and they have made Buddha very rational. He was not so. You cannot be if you are deep into existence. You have to be irrational many times. And a Buddha is! But to know this, we have to put aside the whole tradition and encounter Buddha directly. It is very difficult, but it can happen.

If I am talking to a rational person, unconsciously he discards all that is not rational. But if I am talking to a poet, the same sentence and the same words signify something different. A rational man cannot look at the poetry of the words. He can look only at the logic, the argument. A poet sees the words in a different way. The words have a shade of color, a poetry that is not connected at all with any argument.

So the faces of Buddha differ according to the person who is seeing him. Buddha existed in India in a period when the whole country was going through a crisis of everything irrational: the Vedas, the Upanishads, the whole mysticism. The movement against all this was very great, particularly in Bihar where Buddha was.

Buddha was charismatic, hypnotic. People were impressed by him. But the interpretation of Buddha was bound to be rational. If Buddha had lived at another time in history, in a part of the world that was not against mysticism, he would have been seen as a great mystic, not as an intellectual. The face that is known belongs to the history of a particular time.

As I see Buddha, he was not primarily rational. The whole concept of nirvana is mystical. He was even more mystical than the Upanishads, because the Upanishads, however mystical they look, have their own rationality. They talk about transmigration of the soul. Buddha talked about transmigration *without* a soul. It is more mystical. The Upanishads talk about liberation, but *you* will be there. Otherwise, the whole thing becomes nonsense. If "I" cannot be in that ultimate state of existence, then the whole effort is useless, illogical. Buddha said the effort is to be done . . . and you will not be there. It will just be nothingness. The concept is more mystical.

When you talk about people regressing, do you mean regressing in comparison to some image that has been created by the society of what is socially acceptable?

Not an image. Something different. When I say they are behaving like children, I mean they are not growing. They are regressing, moving backward. I do not have any image of what they should conform to. I have a concept of growth, not an image to be followed. I do not want people to become adjusted to a particular image at all. What I am saying is only that they are regressing back to the past and not growing toward the future. I have no image of how I want the tree to grow. But it must grow; it must not regress. It is a question of growth or regression, not of any image.

Secondly, when I say they are regressing, I mean they are reacting against a too rational society. Their reaction goes to the other extreme. It contains the same fallacy. Reason must be absorbed, not left out. If you leave it out, you are committing the same error as when irrationality is left out.

The Victorian era created a man who was just a facade, a mask. He was not a living being inside. He was a pattern of behavior, a pattern of mannerisms. More a face and less a being. This was possible because we chose only reason to be the criterion of everything. The irrational, the anarchic, the chaotic, was pushed away, suppressed. Now that the anarchic side is taking revenge, it can do two things: it can be destructive or creative.

If it is destructive then it will be regressive. Then it will take revenge in the same manner—by denying. It will deny the rational part. Then you become just like children: immature. You go backward. If the anarchic side is creative, it must not commit the same error. It must absorb reason along with the irrational. Then the whole being will grow. Neither one who has denied the irrational nor one who has denied the rational is growing. You cannot grow unless you grow totally. I am talking about growth. I have no image of what one must grow into.

Aren't a lot of the problems of the Western mind the result of the sin-and-guilt in Christianity?

Yes, that is bound to be. The concept of sin creates a very different consciousness around it. This concept is lacking in the Eastern mind. Rather, it is substituted for by the concept of ignorance. In Eastern consciousness the root of all evil is ignorance not sin. Evil is there because you are ignorant. So the problem is not of guilt but of discipline. You have to be more aware, more knowing. In the East, knowledge is transformation—and meditation is the instrument for that transformation.

With Christianity, sin became the center. And it is not only *your* sin. It is the original sin of humanity. You are burdened with a concept of sin. This creates guilt, tension. That is why Christianity could not really develop meditative techniques. It only developed prayer. What can you do to fight sin? You can be moral and prayerful!

There is nothing like the Ten Commandments in the East. An overly moral concept is not there. So the problems in the East are different from the West. With people who come from the West, guilt is the problem. Deep down they feel guilty. Even those who have revolted feel guilty. It is a psychological problem, concerned more with the mind and less with the being.

First, their guilt has to be released. That is why the East had to develop psychoanalysis and confession. They were not developed in the East because they were never needed. In the West you have to confess. Only then can you get free from the guilt that is deep inside. Or you have to go through psychoanalysis so that the guilt is thrown out. But it is never thrown own permanently, because the concept of sin remains. The guilt will accumulate again. So psychoanalysis and confession can only be a temporary help. You have to confess again and again. They are only temporary helps against something that has been accepted. The root of the disease—the concept of sin—has been accepted.

In the East it is not a question of psychology. It is a question of being. It is not a question of mental health. Rather, it is a question of spiritual growth. You have to grow spiritually, to be more aware of things. You do not have to change your behavior, but to change your consciousness. Then the behavior follows.

Christianity is more concerned with your behavior. But behavior is just peripheral. The question is not what you do; the question is what you are. If you go on changing what you are doing, you are not really changing anything. You remain the same. You can be a saint outwardly and still be the same being inside.

The problem of those coming from the West is because of the guilt they have about their behavior. I have to struggle with them just to make them aware of their deeper problem—which is of the being, not of the psyche.

Buddhism and Jainism have also created guilt. Not the same kind of guilt, but guilt in a different way. Jains in particular have created a very deep feeling of inferiority. Guilt in the Christian sense is not there because there is no question of sin, but there is a deep feeling that unless one goes beyond certain things, one is inferior. This deep inferiority works in the same way as guilt.

Jains have not created any meditative techniques either. They have only created different formulas: "do that," "do that," "don't do this." The whole concept is centered around behavior. A Jain monk is ideal as far as his behavior is concerned, but as far as his inner being is concerned he is very poor. He goes on behaving just like a puppet. That is why Jainism has become a dead thing.

Buddhism is not dead in the same way because a different emphasis is there. The ethical part of Buddhism is just a consequence of the meditative part. If behavior has to be changed, it is just as a help to meditation. In itself, it is meaningless. In Christianity and Jainism it is meaningful in itself. If you are doing good, then you *are* good. For Buddhism this is not the case. You have to be transformed inwardly. Doing good can help, it can become a part, but meditation is the center.

So of the three, only Buddhists have developed deep meditation. Everything else in Buddhism is just a help—not significant. You can even discard it. If you can meditate without any other help, then you can discard the rest.

But Hinduism is even deeper. That is why Hinduism could develop in so many different dimensions, like tantra. Even what you call sin can be used by tantra. Hinduism is, in a way, very healthy. But chaotic of course. Anything healthy is bound to be chaotic; it cannot be systematized.

Rajneesh Meditation Centers in the United States

Ananda, 29 East 28th Street, New York, N.Y. 10016. 212-686-3261

Bodhitaru, 7231 S.W. 62nd Place, Miami, Florida 33143.

Sarvam, 6412 Luzon Avenue, Washington, D.C. 20012. 202-726-1712

Geetam, Box 576, Highway 18, Lucerne Valley, California 92356. 714-248-6163

Paras, 4301 24th Street, San Francisco, California 94122. 415-664-6600

Premsagar, P.O. Box 2862, Chapel Hill, North Carolina 27514.

Rajneesh Yoga Institute, 3910 El Cajon Blvd., San Diego, California 92115

Batohi c/o Esalen Institute, Big Sur, California 93920. 408-667-2335

Dhyanataru, 375A Huron Avenue, Cambridge, Massachusetts 02138

Shantiduta, P.O. Box 52911, Houston, Texas 77052. 713-527-9039

Devagar, 310 Petit Brule, Ste. Madeleine de Regand, P.O. J0P 1 P0

About the Author

Bhagwan Shree Rajneesh is one of India's most widely known and widely respected spiritual masters. He is also one of the most revolutionary and controversial. Like other great enlightened masters of the past—Buddha, Mahavir, Christ, Lao Tzu, Patanjali, Eckhart—his teaching is absolutely contemporary. The words he uses, and the techniques he devises, are specifically tailored to meet the needs of the thousands of spiritual seekers from all over the world who come to him for guidance.

Because Bhagwan has no one path, every spiritual path is his. In his daily morning discourses at his ashram in Poona, India, Bhagwan speaks on the scriptures of every religious tradition, bringing them to life again for us so that we can understand their original meaning, and their relevancy for us today. He is not combining all the religions into one new whole. Rather, he is using the various traditions to bring one to the essence of religiousness—a religiousness that is not concerned with sects, with dogma, with ritual.

Bhagwan's approach is psychological not philosophical, existential not theoretical. The meditation techniques that he has devised start out from a psychotherapeutic base since that is where most of us must begin from today. In addition to daily meditation sessions (and intensive meditation camps that take place from the 11th to the 20th of every month), thirty to forty therapy and meditation groups take place monthly at the ashram in Poona. These include: encounter groups, primal therapy, gestalt, enlightenment intensives, massage workshops, music groups, t'ai chi, yoga, hypnotherapy, sufi dancing, bioenergetics, mime, chanting, tantra workshops, centering, counseling training, energy workshops, vipassana meditation, and various groups that have developed at the ashram and are unique to it. Individual therapy and body work (massage, rolfing, alexander technique, shiatsu, postural integration, polarity balancing, primal therapy and personal counseling) are also available. All of the groups, traditional and neo-traditional, are led by trained therapists from the West, under Bhagwan's guidance.

Over twenty-five new books by Bhagwan are published every year in India. Meditation techniques devised by Bhagwan are taught at Rajneesh centers throughout the world.

For more information, write or visit Shree Rajneesh Ashram, 17 Koregaon Park, Poona, Maharastra, India.